G000321160

· POPULAR ·
· COLLECTABLES ·

lamps and lighting

Josie A. Marsden

GUINNESS PUBLISHING

Dedication

For my daughter, Natalie
with love

Project Editor: Honor Head
Editor: Beatrice Frei
Picture Research: Julie O'Leary
Design and Layout: Steve Leaning
Photographer: Peter Greenhalf

Published in Great Britain by Guinness
Publishing Ltd,
33 London Road, Enfield, Middlesex

Typeset in Caslon Old Style
by Ace Filmsetting Ltd, Frome
Printed and bound in Italy
by New Interlitho SpA, Milan

**British Library Cataloguing in
Publication Data**
Marsden, Josie A.
  Popular collectables, lamps and lighting.
  1. Lamps – Collectors' guides
  I. Title
  749'.63

ISBN 0-85112-905-6

contents

introduction

This book is intended as an informative guide for the collector and buyer of antique and period lamps. It deals primarily with the period 1800–1940 and is divided into sections dealing with the four main light sources: candle, oil, gas and electricity. Each section starts with a short history and then developments are arranged chronologically, followed by styles divided into categories of ceiling, wall, floor, table and lampshades. This is to facilitate planning complete lighting schemes in any given style.

There is an interesting illustrated list of the leading Art Nouveau and Art Deco designers and manufacturers of light fittings. Whereas their lamps may appear on the market infrequently, and fetching such high prices as to be out of reach of the majority of us, the styles that they originated were often copied and can still be found at more reasonable prices. At the end of the book is an extensive glossary of antique lighting terminology and nomenclature, and a comprehensive index for easy reference.

Price guides have been given where applicable, but it must be stressed that they are only guidelines. Prices can be affected by so many things including: age, condition, size, fashion, colour, supply and demand, where you buy, and whether two people at an auction are determined to have the item. Lamps are not automatically valuable because they are old. Two 1930s table lamps sold for similar prices when new could be worth vastly different amounts today, due entirely to fashion or desirability. Lamps and lighting fixtures which are unrestored and not in working order may have vital parts missing, but they will be much cheaper than those offered for sale fully restored and wired ready for use. Most people

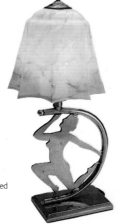

ABOVE: One of a pair of carved giltwood and gesso wall lights, c. 1920. £195–£325
RIGHT: Art Deco white metal lady with marbled glass shade, c. 1930. £135–£165

French three-arm painted
iron chandelier with
entwined leaves and tulips,
c.1912. £195–£295

who buy antique light fittings want to put them to practical use, so remember, a bargain is not a real bargain if the item is unusable.

I would like to thank all the people who have worked so hard to make this book a success, especially my editor Beatrice Frei and photographer Peter Greenhalf. Special thanks are also due to Iris Wood and Linda North, Diana and John for finding me so many of the lovely lamps featured in this book and for their constant support and encouragement.

My appreciation also goes to all those who have given me their help often at short notice; Maggie Blockley, Valerie Frost, Ruth Leveson, Maev Alexander, Nadine Hanson at Harrods, Stella Beddoe at Brighton Museum, Ron Miles, Mr Angove; Barbara Needham and last but not least my husband, Cedric.

Josie A. Marsden, Magic Lanterns Antique Lighting, at By George, 23 George Street, St Albans, Herts.

candles

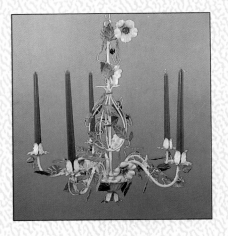

Five-arm painted tinware chandelier.

early history

From the beginning of time man has sought to find a way to lighten the darkness of night, which has always been feared as it conceals all kinds of dangers, and yet almost half of our lives are spent in its darkness.

The early cave dwellers found that their wood fires not only warmed them but provided some useful light and kept the wild animals at bay. In fact for more than 30 000 years the domestic fire was the only source of illumination for the majority of people in all parts of the world. It has continued to be used as the principal source of light in the home for thousands of years, long after oil lamps, gas lights and even electricity were discovered.

Ecclesiastical 18th-century iron chandelier for candles, converted to electricity with imitation wooden candles.
£400–£600

· SPLINT ·
· LAMPS ·

The first portable lights were simply blazing pieces of wood plucked from the fire, and wedged into fissures in the rocks. The earliest candles were made from wood split into thin pieces (splints) for easier combustion. Special devices held the individual splints vertically or horizontally or provided a small bowl in which to burn a small quantity of them.

· FIRE · BASKETS ·

From the times of the ancient pharaohs of Alexandria, iron baskets and bronze bowls filled with fire and attached to long poles, or fixed to the wall, were called fire baskets or cressets. They were used outside buildings, for ceremonial occasions, and in lighthouses. Versions of these were still made as recently as the 18th century.

Bog pine, popular in Elizabethan Britain, was particularly good for illumination as it was full of turpentine. Split and dried, it was often used instead of candles wherever there was a plentiful supply.

· RUSH · LIGHTS ·

From medieval times and earlier, rushes were made into a type of candle. The rushes, gathered in early autumn, were peeled, leaving one or two strips to support the soft pithy centre. They were then dried and dipped in tallow. The tallow wall was quite thin, but a rush light 2½feet long would burn for about an hour. Rush lights were more economical than tallow candles and they did not need snuffing as did candles when charred pieces of the wick had to be cut off and removed about every half-hour. Eleven rushes giving about half an hour's light each (5½ hours' light altogether) could be purchased for a farthing (there were 960 farthings in £1) whereas a halfpenny (480 to £1) tallow candle might burn for about 2 hours. Either way lighting was expensive.

· CANDLES ·

Candles have been used for lighting churches, municipal and domestic dwellings for over 2000 years but there

Victorian ecclesiastical brass candle lamp.
£195–£375

Victorian three-arm iron and turned oak chandelier. £150–£350

is no reliable information about the use of candles in England until around the 10th century AD. Historians generally believe that the Romans introduced them into Britain, and from Saxon times artificial lighting was predominantly by candles.

During the Middle Ages the chandler (candlemaker) became an important and stalwart member of the community and the art of his craft developed steadily. Candles were made either of wax (beeswax) or tallow, which was a mixture of glycerides, including stearic, palmitic and oleic acids and extracted chiefly from the suet of sheep and cattle. Any leftover fat was used for tallow candles or rush lights and frequently this was an edible fat. Wax candles were always used in churches and by those who could afford them, as they kept their shape and gave a cleaner, brighter light with less guttering. Tallow was much cheaper but far softer and always needed to be set in a candle cup. Tallow candles would often give as good a light as those made of wax but only for about 10 minutes,

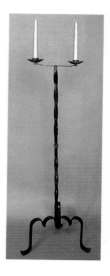

18th-century iron tripod-leg floor candelabra. £195–£450

then the light would gradually grow dimmer and dimmer. They were also smoky, messy, guttered easily and smelt very unpleasant.

By mid-Victorian times (*c.* 1880) tallow candles were about 12 times, and spermaceti nearly 30 times as costly as gas (using an Argand burner) for an equal intensity of light.

It was not until 1820 that the Frenchman Cambacères discovered that by plaiting the cotton wick instead of twisting it, it would bend over into the flame as the candle burned and be consumed like the rush stems, thereby producing a snuffless candle. In 1831 it was found that if boric acid was allowed to impregnate the plaited wick, 'guttering' was also eliminated.

Candles remained the main source of domestic light (apart from firelight) well into the 20th century in spite of the advance and popularity of gas and oil lighting. By Edwardian times they were made in all manner of sizes and materials and for all occasions. Elblana, Ozokerit and Patent wax were advised as best for carriage lamps, whereas spermaceti, planet sperm, parastrine shade and whitehall sperm were recommended for use in Arctic lamps and other spring-loaded candle lamps or candles requiring shades when a full upright candle was needed.

Candlesticks and the evolution of their design through the ages is an extensive subject with very many different styles and therefore only those items that can be called candle lamps have been included.

Arts and Crafts triangular iron three-light chandelier with fancy chain.
£165–£295

ceiling

· CHANDELIERS ·

Early candle holders consisted of iron
spikes or prickets set in crude wooden
beams called candle beams which were
the forerunners of chandeliers. They
could also be mounted on squares or
circles of iron and suspended on chains.
These continued to be made well into
the 19th century. Only wax candles can
be used on prickets as tallow candles are
far too soft and need a candle socket to
support them. Iron and wood candle
chandeliers were frequently used in
churches and inns and some country
houses. Their simplicity gives them a
special charm and today they look most
effective in country-style kitchens,
breakfast and family rooms. They are
also most effective in barn and stable
conversions as well as cottages. They
can be converted to electricity but they
look wonderful with candles as they give
a warm ambience to the room. Circular
iron chandeliers can be used to display
kitchenware or bunches of herbs or
dried flowers suspended on meat hooks.
At Christmas time they can be entwined
with holly and laurel.

Early ironwork was always forged by
hand and careful examination of old iron
chandeliers will show irregularities only
found in handmade articles.

Victorian circular wrought
iron three-light chandelier.
£135–£295

Dutch-style five-arm brass
chandelier c.1920.
£145–£275

Victorian Rise and Fall candle lamp with original ruby glass. Note the brass weight and pulleys that enabled the lamp to be pulled down for lighting and extinguishing.
£195–£495

Early Victorian Rise and Fall pendant lamp for one candle, with ornate rose glass shade, hand painted and gilded and inset with coloured cut glass jewels.
£275–£550

Many of the chandeliers were converted (often rather badly) to electricity in the 1920s, but it is usually fairly easy to reconvert them for candle use. They must have a candle cup or pricket and a drip tray if they are to be used for candles. Lack of cups and drip trays does not necessarily mean that the item is of a later date, as they may have been taken off when the electrical conversion was done; but it is an indication that you should look at the whole of the item more carefully, to check its age.

By the 17th century wealthy and titled people had candle chandeliers finely made in bronze as well as steel, wood and iron. These became very elaborate, and were made in crystal glass, gilded wood, gilded iron, as well as ormolu in the 18th and 19th centuries. Most of these chandeliers are now in museums. Occasionally they are sold at auctions for thousands of pounds.

In Victorian England and well into the 20th century, while the horse remained one of the principal modes of transport, every town and village had a local blacksmith. Many of these blacksmiths were skilled craftsmen who produced beautiful household artifacts in iron, including lamps. In France and Italy, at the turn of the century, artist/craftsmen forged delightful objects, beautiful flowers, leaves and animals in iron which they painted in Provençal colours and made into chandeliers, wall, table and floor lamps for candles and electricity. Sometimes the fine ironwork was gilded and looked very grand.

Painted or gilded iron chandeliers fashioned with entwined flowers and leaves look delightful in a lounge, conservatory or garden room, and add a wonderfully extravagant air to the bathroom.

· SCONCES ·

Ever since candles were invented, people have been trying to find ways to improve their illumination. It was soon noticed that if candles were placed in front of a mirror or a brightly polished surface, the amount of light thrown out was greatly magnified. Therefore mirrors were fitted with one or more candleholders in front of them. Also, wall sconces for candles frequently had large backplates of polished bronze or copper, often with attractive designs on them. These sconces make lovely decorative items for lounges, hall, bathroom or bedrooms. Although very early examples are hard to find and prohibitively expensive for the average collector, many Victorian and Edwardian examples can be found at reasonable prices. Often these were made in the styles of earlier centuries. The most valuable ones are those that retain their original mirrors, even if the silvering shows signs of wear.

Regency ormolu two-arm candle sconce with classical relief picture.
£150–£400

· GIRANDOLES ·

It is worth looking for pairs of these ornamental wall candleholders as they are very collectable and hold their value very well, but even a single one can look most effective if placed at the end of a hall, in a small cloakroom or in a niche or archway. They were made in many styles and materials. The most sought after are those in Rococo style in ormolu or giltwood. The Victorians commonly framed their mirrors with velvet, which can look most effective if tied in with the overall colour scheme. Other girandoles have relief pictures in bronze, brass or copper as the backplate. Use the mirrored candleholders

Art Nouveau repoussé brass two-light candle sconce. This sconce is over 2ft high.

18th-century brass three-arm candle sconce.
£150–£350

wherever the candlelight needs to be maximised. A pair on one wall of the dining room gives gentle flattering reflections when dining by candlelight. Wall sconces for candles are becoming very popular for dining rooms. In a small room, the candles will give background heating as well as a warm, friendly ambience, and leave the table clear for all the gourmet goodies.

· CARRIAGE ·
· LAMPS ·

Candles were also used in carriage lamps. Old brass carriage lamps are in great demand today for use as outside lights. It is far more difficult to find pairs of these than the odd single one. Usually they have been converted to electricity; very few people use them with candles except on boats and yachts, but they add a grand touch placed either side of the front door, entrance gates, or in a porch. Carriage lamps were also made in cast iron and other metals. They can look effective when used for lighting halls, passages and stairways.

One of a pair of Victorian brass carriage lamps, now converted to electricity. Note decorative brass swags across the glass panes. Pair £295–£400

· TORCHÈRES ·

Candles were also displayed on floor-standing constructions – the forerunners of our standard lamps. The earliest examples were made of iron or wood. They could be for one or two candles or as many as 18 or 20, usually arranged in a row, circle or stepped sequence. From the 17th to the 19th century very elaborate torchères were made in carved giltwood, bronze and ormolu which were mounted on large marble plinths.

Torchères most freqently found in antique shops are those made of iron or iron and wood, which were originally used in churches and chapels. These can still be purchased fairly reasonably and look stunning in barn conversions and Elizabethan houses, but they can also be used effectively in reception halls, dining rooms, kitchens and conservatories. The best torchères for practical use are the heaviest as they cannot be knocked over.

Ecclesiastical iron floor candelabra with brass nozzles and cups for 18 candles. Early 20th century. £550–£750

Sheffield plate candlestick lamp with Arctic fitting and hallmarked silver filigree Goram candle shade.
£100–£200

· CANDLESTICK ·
· LAMPS ·

From 1770 a candlestick lamp was manufactured which was adapted from a bedroom candlestick to provide a lamp which would give a steady flame, even in draughty places. It had a metal base of silver, brass or bronze and a high glass funnel which slotted into the base. The metal body below the funnel was pierced to create an upward draught of air. Sometimes these candle lamps had glass globes instead of funnels to protect the flame. The candle was often enclosed in a spring device to keep it at the same height as it burned. This fitment was adapted to wall candleholders for railway carriages.

· STUDENT ·
· LAMPS ·

Scholars who studied by candlelight often used a screen attached to the candle to protect their eyes from the brightness of the flickering flame, without obstructing the light on the page of their book. These screens were called candleshields and were commonly made of a reflective material to maximise the available light. The first candleshield was patented in 1817.

A form of student lamp appeared in the 18th century which became so popular that it remained in use until Edwardian times. It was a metal candle lamp with a hooded metal reflector which concentrated the light on the books being read. The candle was spring-loaded in a metal tube, so that it remained at the same height even though the wax melted away as it burned. By 1913 this lamp was so successful that a cheap version in nickel plate, called the Holborn Candle

Victorian brass spring-loaded Student lamp with hooded metal reflector. This style first appeared in the 18th century and remained popular until the early 20th century.

Reading Lamp, could be purchased for only 3s 11d (20p). Some reflector lamps had an eye screen attachment to prevent the eyes having to deal with the flickering flame, and others were telescopic so that the height could be adjusted to suit the student or the task.

In their 1895/6 catalogue, Harrods show an interesting double reading light for candles, which looks very similar to the Double Queens Reading Lamp made for oil. The lamp has a central pole with carrying loop and a candle positioned on either side. Each candle is shaded by an opal glass dome similar to that used on oil lamps. On the same page, a Railway Reading Lamp for candles is shown with a simple reflector and a pneumatic sucker to stick it on the carriage window – and all this for just 3s 3d (16p).

Victorian double reading lamp for candles in brass in opal glass dome shades. The base is well weighted and there is a central carrying handle.

· ARCTIC · & · · POLALITE · · LAMPS ·

Candles could be converted to candle lamps by attaching metal, silk, parchment, card or paper shades to them. These protected the candle from draughts so that it gave a steady unflickering light. The problem with these candle lamps was that, as the candle burned, the shade had to be constantly adjusted to keep the same comparative height as the candle or it would catch fire. Devices were developed that kept the candle at the same height while it burned and also supported the shade. One such device was Green's Patent Arctic Lamp for Candles; an Edwardian advertisement describes it thus:

'The Arctic Lamp is constructed on the same principle as a carriage or

Arctic lamp in Victorian brass candlestick with goffered linen, beaded candle shade.

Polalite candle tube cross-section, with china cup which keeps the candle cool and prevents guttering. The socket is india rubber and adjusts to fit any ordinary candlestick.

Regency ormolu candlestick with dog and hunting horn, converted to electricity with Victorian lace and silk, beaded shade. £195–£255

reading lamp, in which the candle, enclosed in a metal tube, is forced up as it burns by means of a spiral spring inside. It fits in any ordinary candlestick and is made to resemble a wax candlestick when in use. Ordinary candle shades can be used with perfect safety. The candles always remain the same height, yet are burned to the end without the slightest waste.' Polalite lamps were a similar design to Arctic lamps.

· NIGHT · · LIGHTS ·

In the 19th century many different candle lights were made, including a large number of night lights. The latter consisted of a glass dish on a pedestal to hold the candle, with a glass cover to protect the flame. Some of the covers were etched or painted with domestic scenes whereas others used coloured glass. One of the manufacturers, Samuel Clarke of London, introduced in 1860 a special slow-burning safety candle for night lights. He used a fairy with a wand as his trade mark and some of his lights bear the words 'Fairy Light' or 'Pyramid'. This is how Christmas lights have become known as fairy lights. Other night lights were made like little pottery cottages with windows, doors, an open front and a chimney. These were made in Staffordshire and at Rockingham. They are much sought after by collectors.

· CANDLE · · SHADES ·

Candle shades were freqently fitted to candles to protect them from draughts; this helped to prevent flickering and guttering, thereby providing a more even light.

In Victorian and Edwardian times these shades were very decorative. They were made of metal, silk, card, vellum, linen and even crêpe paper. Often they were made at home by the ladies of the house.

To prevent the candle burning them, they had to be used with special devices which kept the candle and the shade at the same relative position to each other. The candle was held in position by a spring and the devices were called Arctic or Polalite.

Early Victorian, French ormolu and crystal candelabra, converted to electricity with lined silk georgette shades. £185–£235

· LACEMAKERS' · · LAMPS ·

People who wanted to perform delicate and intricate tasks at night, such as lacemakers, embroiderers, jewellers, goldsmiths and engravers, sought ways of increasing the illumination of candles. The lacemaker's lamp, used by all of the above, consisted of a small table with an adjustable candlestick for a tallow candle in the centre. The tallow candle was surrounded by four

Victorian gilded brass fairy candlestick on large green onyx base, probably originally part of a clock garniture, now converted to a table lamp.

candlesticks, each containing a spherical glass bowl instead of candles. The bowls were filled with water to which distilled spirit was added to keep the water clear and free from algae. The light from the single candle was thus diffused and magnified through the water-filled bowls to give a steady, even and bright light for a number of people around the table to work by. Later, more elaborate versions of this lamp were made, using cut crystal glass to reflect the rays and multiply the light.

· CANDLE ·
· CLOCKS ·

Candles were used to tell the time. The Saxon King Alfred had candles made of established weights and lengths. Each candle was marked with 12 divisions, each division represented 20 minutes, so that each candle burned for 4 hours (240 minutes) and 6 candles made up 1 day. Charles V of France always had a time candle in his chapel that would last the full 24 hours.

· CANDLE ·
· LANTERNS ·

The necessity of protecting candle flames from the wind and of preventing fires should the candle be knocked over encouraged the development of lanterns. Large and small, they were used in stables, farm buildings, outhouses, warehouses, city streets, squares, churches and chapels as well as indoors in corridors and stairways. Panes of glass protected the candle. Sometimes metal fretwork windows or thin translucent horn replaced the glass, being more durable and less likely to break.

Ships candle lantern made of brass. £75–£125

oil

Victorian spelter oil lamp made by Zimmerman & Co.
London but manufactured in Germany. £95–£150

Oil was the first fuel used for lighting, long before candles were invented. Many different oils were employed but until the 18th century all gave a poor light.

Early-Victorian brass Regency-style single flat-wick oil lamp with dome shade. £95–£185

· FLOAT-WICK ·
· LAMPS ·

The earliest lamps consisted of a simple saucer or cone-shaped container without a groove or spout for the wick, which merely floated on the surface of the oil.

Frequently the oil floated on a bed of water, so that the flame always appeared at the same level – high up for better diffusion of light. Float-wick lamps were widely adopted throughout the world and remained in common use well into the 18th century. In eastern mosques and synagogues they were still used in the early 20th century – in some places even today.

· FIRST ·
· DECORATIVE ·
· LAMPS ·

Many Greek and Roman lamps were multi-spouted and made to hang from ceilings, or were mounted on plinths which were adjustable. Everyday lamps, similar to the well-known Aladdin's Lamp, were made in pottery and lead. Wonderfully elaborate lamps of bronze, alabaster, marble, brass, silver and pottery were made in the shapes of gods, birds and animals.

Very few examples of early Egyptian lamps have survived, but it is believed that they primarily used those of the float-wick type. A beautiful alabaster lamp which was at first thought to be a vase, was found in Tutankhamun's tomb in 1926. It had a double bowl with a picture painted on the inner bowl which was only visible when illuminated internally.

Interesting Messengers' oil lamp which fits into a candlestick. The milk glass reservoir is shaped like a candle. £150–£195

· WICKS ·

Until the late 18th century oil lamps changed very little. A simple round cord wick was used. It could not be too thick, otherwise the cord would not burn in the centre but would smoulder and smoke unpleasantly. The first important improvement happened when Monsieur Leger introduced the first flat wick of woven cotton in 1773.

Small Victorian simple round-cord wick oil lamp in silver plate, missing glass chimney. £15–£45

developments

The Crusie.

· THE · CRUSIE ·

The Crusie and variations of it were simple iron-age oil lamps commonly used for hundreds of years, until the early 20th century. The Crusie consisted of a pear-shaped or oval iron bowl with a long handle curving back over the bowl. This could be suspended from a spike or a hook. Sometimes they had two bowls – the lower one to catch drips from the main oil-containing bowl; or the main bowl had a hinged lid attached to it.

This useful lamp was introduced to America by the European settlers and became known as the Betty or Phoebe lamp.

Brass Venetian Reading Lamp (Lucerna) with wick cleaning and trimming implements attached by chains. £45–£125

· THE · LUCERNA ·

This lamp, also called a Venetian Reading Lamp, was a brass table lamp with three spouts that could be adjusted to move up and down a central column. At the top of the column it had a carrying handle. It was very popular in Italy, the Netherlands and other parts of Southern Europe during the 18th and 19th centuries.

· THE · ARGAND · · LAMP ·

A major breakthrough in the light-giving qualities of lamps was made when Amie Argand, a Swiss scientist working in Paris, patented his lamp in 1783. He had experimented with Leger's flat wick which he bent into a cylindrical shape and placed between two metal tubes. A current of air was allowed to pass through the inner tube to the inside of the flame, thereby increasing its brilliance. When his partner

Quinquet held the neck of a broken glass bottle over the wick the increased brightness was quite dramatic. It was the birth of the glass chimney. Both these principles, the value of an upward draught and a chimney around the flame, to increase the power of the flame, were in fact discovered by Leonardo da Vinci nearly 300 years earlier, although Leonardo's chimney was made of metal, not glass. The new Argand lamp gave 12 times as much light as any previous lamp had done.

The Argand lamp burned colza, carcel or rape-seed oil which was obtained from brassica (cabbages, kale and rape). This oil gave a good light but was so sticky and heavy that it did not easily soak its way up the wick by capillary action. Furthermore the flame varied as the level of oil in the reservoir changed. To overcome this problem the reservoir was placed higher than the wick, to get a bird fountain feed effect with the oil being supplied to the wick by gravity and regulated by a valve. However, these lamps had a very high oil consumption, so were expensive to run. The high reservoir created inconvenient shadows and tended to make the lamps top heavy.

· QUEEN'S · · READING · · LAMP ·

This design was introduced for burning colza oil about 1830. It consisted of a central brass pole with a carrying handle and a crossbar. The cylindrical reservoir on one side was counterbalanced by the lamp and glass shade on the opposite side. The crossbar sloped downwards from the reservoir to the wick. The lamp was adjustable in height and had a dome-shaped shade over the funnel,

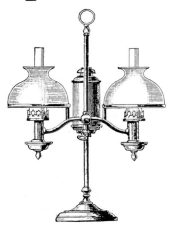

Double Queen's Reading Lamp in brass with opal glass dome shades c.1895. This design was originally introduced for colza oil c.1830. £225–£500

often coloured green, to reduce glare. Oil was fed to the wick by a dispenser mechanism. There were two float valves in the reservoir, an upper and lower valve and an air hole. As a little air entered the reservoir, the equivalent amount of oil flowed out. The oil could not drop from the upper reservoir unless air replaced it, otherwise a vacuum would have formed.

This elegant design was so successful that it survived for nearly 100 years and was quickly adapted to burn paraffin when it became cheap and widely available. It became known as a Queen's Reading Lamp, and double and single versions were available. The style is still popular today and reproductions adapted to run on electricity are sold.

·THE·CARCEL· ·LAMP·

Colza or carcel oil, although heavy and sticky, was safe and easy to store without deterioration. It gave a clear, odourless and nearly smokeless flame, so much thought was given to the problem of getting the oil to the wick. As capillary action was not effective, Carcel invented a clockwork pump (*c.* 1800) which forced the oil up to an Argand wick, and allowed any excess oil to flow back into the main reservoir. Carcel lamps gave a steady bright light for seven or eight hours if properly managed, but the mechanism was easily disturbed and they consumed oil at an alarming rate.

Throughout the 19th century there was a flood of inventions. After thousands of years of very little change in domestic illumination, it was as if man thought for the first time about how he could make improvements. The most important developments in oil lamps follow.

· THE · BUDE · · LAMP ·

This was basically an Argand lamp with oxygen passed into it to obtain a brighter flame. It was later adapted to burn coal gas.

· THE · · DRUMMOND · · LAMP ·

An intense light was produced by feeding the flame with a jet of oxygen, while it was in contact with lime, hence the origin of limelight.

· THE · · MODERATOR · · LAMP ·

This was another improvement on the Argand lamp, and was patented by a

Frenchman, Franchot, in 1835. The oil was stored in the body of the lamp and propelled up the wick by a strong spiral spring on a leather piston. The spring was wound up by a rack and pinion and the flow was regulated by a tapering rod in the ascending tube, called the 'moderator'. This lamp was extremely popular in France, well into the 20th century.

· THE · DIACON · · LAMP ·

An American lamp produced *c.* 1840 which worked on the same principle as the earlier Carcel lamp.

· THE · · OLEOSTATIC · · LAMP ·

Oleostatic lamps were lamps that used hydraulic principles. By an arrangement of chambers, brine and oil were displaced, thereby forcing the oil to the wick.

· LUCIGEN, · · DOTY · & · · WELLS · LAMPS ·

In these lamps, the oil was forced by high pressure from the reservoir through a spiral heated by the flame of the lamp. The heated oil was ejected partly as a vapour and partly as a fluid. It burnt as a large, highly luminous flame. This principle survives today in contractors' flare lamps of the Wells type.

· WHALE · OIL · · LAMPS ·

Lamps designed to burn whale oil,

Well's Patent Hurricane lamp with mica windows around the burner. In 1899 this lamp cost 6s 6d (32½p). £30–£65

usually had a single vertical wick, and gave a light comparable to that obtained from colza and rape-seed oil.

· CAMPHENE ·
· LAMPS ·

Popular in the USA between 1830–50, these lamps had two wicks and burnt a volatile mixture of camphene (crystalline terpene – turpentine) and alcohol. When not in use the wicks had to be covered with special wick caps to prevent the fuel evaporating. They had wide bases to help prevent accidental overturning; but there were still numerous disastrous fires from the use of these lamps, because of the volatile nature of their fuel. They were not popular in Europe as they were considered too dangerous.

Brass whale oil lamp with single wick, 14in high.
£78–£98

· NAPHTHA ·

Naphtha was distilled from coal and gave brilliant illumination, which was particularly useful outdoors when lighting large areas. Naphtha was used for lamps as early as the 17th century. The poet John Milton wrote that 'naphtha and asphaltum burnt together yielded light like the sky'.

· THE ·
· HOLLIDAY ·
· LAMP ·

A new type of naphtha lamp was developed in the mid-19th century, called the Holliday lamp. It had a wickless burner. The fuel supply was controlled by a needle valve, and the oil was vaporised through the heat of the flame and burned through small orifices

developments

in a rose burner. In order to start the lamp it had to be heated by burning methylated spirits. It was extremely successful for outdoor lighting and continued to be used for outdoor street markets for over 100 years.

· PARAFFIN ·

The invention of paraffin paved the way for the blossoming of the great Victorian oil lamp industry. Paraffin is a mixture of liquid hydrocarbons obtained by distilling petroleum (mineral oil) or coal and bitumens. Reichenbach and Christison discovered paraffin in 1830 but it was not until James Young, a Scot, perfected his refining process in 1847 (patented 1850) that real developments were made. His company, Young's Paraffin Oil Company, was later absorbed by the oil giant British Petroleum Company (BP).

This new fuel was far superior to all other lamp oils. The Germans were the first to recognise its potential and the earliest paraffin lamps come from there. But in spite of its superiority, paraffin did not gain immediate popularity, probably because the main supplies of oil came from Burma and Romania and were quite expensive.

It was the discovery of oil in vast quantities in Pennsylvania, USA, in 1859 by 'Colonel' Edwin L. Drake, and the subsequent development of the American oil industry, that changed all that. By the end of 1860 there were 70 oil wells in Pennsylvania and over half a million barrels of oil had been produced. Suddenly, there was a cheap and abundant supply of fuel. For the first time in history there was an inexpensive and effective illuminant for every home that was easily portable and not dependent on a local gas works.

Wizard central draught oil lamp with milk glass base, reservoir and globe. Made in Germany. Height 19½in. £65–£95

The age of the paraffin lamp had arrived and between 1859 and 1870 over 80 patents were taken out every year for new devices to improve the performance of oil lamps.

· THE · DUPLEX ·
· BURNER ·

In 1865 Joseph Hinks, an Englishman, made one of the most important inventions, the Duplex burner. Hinks placed two flat wicks side by side and added an extinguisher device. The two lighted wicks in close proximity produced a flame of greater luminosity than before. So successful was the design of the Duplex burner that it is still produced today, with the basic design virtually unchanged.

Duplex lamps were produced in all styles and sizes for every room and every occasion.

British Duplex burner with Art Nouveau design on cast iron base, brass container and engraved glass shade. Height 18½ in. £95–£150

· CENTRAL ·
· DRAUGHT ·
· BURNER ·

This lamp had a tubular wick with a hollow draught tube in the centre which produced a very efficient flame, with capacities up to 200 candlepower. The central draught lamps had spreaders or air diffusers of many different types fitted on to the central tube. It is worth remembering that the burner will not work if the spreader is missing and it will smoke if the spreader is distorted or broken.

The most popular lamp of the Victorian era was a central draught lamp called Veritas. Many church and municipal lights were also central draught because of their greater illuminating powers. Most church lights would provide at least 100 candlepower.

French central draught burner oil lamp with silver plated base and hand painted and gilded glass reservoir. £75–£150

One of a pair of Kosmos brass oil lamps marked W & W, of Regency design with base of black marble. Converted to electricity. £295–£450

· KOSMOS ·

Kosmos lamps had a flat wick which appeared circular in the burner. The draught was taken from the side of the burner in a similar way to the flat-wick designs and it had no spreader as the central draught types did. Kosmos was used for boudoir reading and small hand lamps.

· WANZER, · · KRANZOW · & · · HITCHCOCK ·

Glass chimneys played an essential part in producing a flame of maximum luminosity but they were very fragile and could not be easily transported. The Wanzer, Kranzow and Hitchcock were all chimneyless lamps that relied on a clockwork-operated fan to drive a current of air round the oil reservoir and up to the wick. They were not as effective as lamps which had a chimney to protect the flame from side draughts but they did have the advantage of being able to be used for cooking over as well as for lighting. However, they were rarely used in the home because of the fire risk. The Hitchcock lamp, patented in 1880, was one of the most successful of this type of oil lamp. These oil lamps were mostly used by travellers, the armed forces and people working out of doors who were frequently on the move.

· THE · · INCANDESCENT · · OIL · LAMP ·

A major breakthrough in increasing the luminosity and candlepower of the flame was made when the incandescent mantle was introduced in 1893. Following earlier experiments by Clamond, Carl Auer von Welsbach of Vienna (a pupil of Bunsen, famous for his gas burner used in thousands of school laboratories) experimented between 1885 and 1893 and developed the incandescent mantle. These mantles could be used for oil or gas lights. They consisted of a silk or cotton fabric impregnated with a mixture containing thorium and cerium. The mantle was then suspended in the flame of an oil or gas lamp. When it was heated to a certain temperature it produced a pleasing glow of high luminosity.

The incandescent mantle was only really successful for oil lamps when used on oil vapour lamps, such as the one introduced by Kitson in 1885. Other lamps had a fuel pump attachment which supplied vaporised fuel under pressure to the mantle. The most famous of these types of lamps were Famos, Aladdin and Tilley. Due to the amazing amount of light they emit, variations of these lamps are still used today for emergency lighting.

Duplex burner lamps could be converted to use the incandescent mantle by exchanging the fitting for a Kronos or Candesco and thereby increasing its candlepower to 80 or 100.

A popular French lamp using the mantle was the Titus, which was fuelled by methylated spirits. Although this was a clean and pleasant fuel, it never became really popular in Britain owing to its cost.

Edwardian brass Tilley lamp with etched glass shade. A fuel pump is housed in the base which supplies vaporised fuel to the incandescent mantle. £40–£95

· PETROL ·
· LAMPS ·

Pressure lamps using a mantle and burning petrol were used extensively in America. The Coleman lamp which originated in Canada was one of the most popular. In Britain, the Petrolite lamp gave a light of 50 candlepower, but it never really caught on as petrol was generally considered a dangerous fuel. There also was a 400-candlepower petrol vapour storm-proof lantern. The Buck and Hickman Ltd catalogue of the time describes them: 'These lanterns burn 95 per cent air with 5 per cent petrol vapour . . . and can be swung or even overturned without harm. The mantles are extremely durable. There is no oil or fuel to spill, but they must not be filled whilst alight. Light with a match.'

Petrolite floor-standing lamps gave an excellent light for reading. The illumination was by petrol vapour and air. In the base of the lamp there was a container with a porous brick. The brick was saturated with a special quality of very light petrol. The fumes that were given off were well diluted with air in the proportion of five parts by volume of petrol vapour to 95 parts by volume of air. This mixture was burnt using an incandescent mantle and when well adjusted apparently gave a very powerful light. The light was usually shaded with a large beaded silk shade.

· PRINCESS ·
· LAMPS ·

These were small oil lamps consisting of a coloured or cut glass reservoir with a central spring toe below the container, which would fit into the cup of a candlestick. Princess lamps were available with a glass chimney and opal glass, linen, silk or paper shades, and they converted candlesticks or sconces into oil lamps. They were often fitted into candle sconces on pianos. They are very pretty and well worth collecting.

A Princess lamp with cut glass reservoir. The spring toe enables it to be fitted into most candlesticks. Harrods Catalogue 1895.

ceiling

· HARP · LAMPS ·

Hanging lamps were made in a variety of sizes and styles. The simplest were harp lamps where the oil reservoir fitted into a metal ring supported by a large pear-shaped metal harp which was hung from the ceiling. Some had reflectors fitted near the top of the harp to reflect the light downwards. All had small smoke bells at the apex of the harp to help protect the ceilings from smoke damage. Harp lamps were available in many different sizes from one-inch slip burners, standard Duplex, 50-candlepower Veritas, Venus etc to the very largest Juno which yielded 200 candlepower. They were mainly used for church halls, schools and public rooms. Today they look most effective and provide a warm light for kitchens, breakfast rooms, dining rooms, as well as small rooms in cottages. Most of the harp lamps with reflectors did not have an additional globe or shade other than the chimney, whereas those without a reflector often had an opal glass dome or Vesta shade. A brass sliding balance ball could be purchased separately. This was used with certain harp lamps to enable them to be lowered for lighting and extinguishing.

Victorian hall lantern in brass frame with leaded cathedral stained glass panels. c.1895. This design was also made for gas. £295–£395

Victorian iron harp lamp with clear glass reservoir, milk glass dome and brass smoke bell. £150–£195

ceiling

· SUSPENSION ·
· LAMPS ·

These were usually quite elaborate, often in cast iron, with a complex arrangement of chains and a weight, so that the lamp could be pulled down to light and extinguish it. Suspension lamps were also made in brass in a variety of finishes and always had shades as well as the glass chimney and smoke bell. The shades were often Vesta or dome-shaped but fancy globes were also used as well as silk and lace shades. Some suspension lamps had a copper leaf reflector (a reflector made of copper in the shape of leaves), constructed in such a way as to render the light shadowless. Smoke bells were made in brass, copper or glass and hung below the weight.

Another type was the vestibule lamp. This was either on a pulley system of a weight and chains or styled in the shape of a lantern with a door or window that could be opened so that the lamp could be lit.

· CHANDELIERS ·

Chandeliers – multi-armed suspensions – for oil were undoubtedly used in grand houses and public buildings. Whereas there are very few featured in British catalogues of the period, the American Sears Roebuck catalogue of *c.* 1895 showed many examples. Probably oil was used more extensively in America than England, due to the cheap paraffin oil available from the Pennsylvanian oil fields. Also, America did not have the same network of gasworks as Britain.

TOP: Victorian Suspension lamp in wrought iron and copper, using a Duplex burner, c.1895.

ABOVE: Thermidor Belge Safety Suspension lamp in polished brass with ivy leaf design, c.1895.

wall and floor

· BRACKET · · LAMPS ·

Wall fittings for oil lamps were called bracket lamps and were used in halls, landings, caravans and railway carriages. Constructed of polished brass, bronzed or oxidised copper and cast iron, they were frequently made to swing from side to side. Brackets fixed in one position were referred to as stiff. Polished brass or mirror glass reflectors were sometimes fitted behind the chimney, to maximise the light. Other brackets had a long curved pole that suspended the smoke pole above them. Discolouration of walls, ceilings and furnishings was a constant problem with oil and gas lighting.

Wrought iron Art Nouveau bracket lamp with copper container and tinted satin glass shade, c.1895.

· STANDARD · · LAMPS ·

Oil standard lamps were very popular. They were usually telescopic so that the height could be adjusted to benefit the individual and direct the light wherever it was particularly needed. They were mostly made in metal, brass, silver plate or iron, or iron with copper embellishments. Occasionally they were made in wood or even bamboo. Often the brass or silver-plated lamps were supplied in an oxidised finish so that they did not need to be polished. They nearly always had large elaborate silk and lace shades with fringes in silk or beads and adorned with bows, rosettes and artificial flowers. The shades frequently cost more than the lamp base itself. Most floor-standing lamps were fitted with a 50-candlepower central draught burner; but incandescent fittings such as those made by Famos were also available.

Edwardian telescopic brass standard lamp converted to electricity with 1920s parchment and velvet shade. £275–£325

table

·DOMESTIC· ·LAMPS·

During Victorian times, even modest
middle-class homes owned many oil
lamps, often one for every room,
whereas a wealthy home might have as
many as 40 lamps. The cleaning and
upkeep of them, filling and trimming
the wicks meant a lot of work for the
servants. The drawing room or parlour
of an ordinary home would have had a
Duplex table lamp with a fancy globe or
a 50-candlepower central draught lamp
in fine china. The dining room probably
had a cheaper version of the parlour
Duplex lamp. The kitchen would
possibly have been lit by a very simple
harp or suspension light as well as one
or two plain brass lamps with a one-inch
flat wick or Kosmos burner without a
globe. Bracket lamps were used in the
toilet or bathroom and in halls and

Victorian brass column oil
lamp with etched glass
globe. Height 23½in.
£95–£155

Brass Students oil lamp
with metal hooded
reflector. £75–£125

passageways. Bedroom lamps consisted of small flat-wick lamps with carrying handles and little night lights for the children. Princess lights were often used in candle sconces on the piano and also provided ideal standby lamps that could be fitted into candlesticks whenever extra illumination was needed.

A transfer-printed opal glass fount on a cast iron base, with a chimney and plain globe, was the cheapest table lamp. A pricier lamp would have had a black china stand and a brass column holding a reservoir of coloured fluted glass. The most expensive lamps were made in silver plate, or brass and copper with cut glass founts and elaborate shades. There were also lamps for special purposes, reading and desk lights, for the library and study, billiard table lights, boudoir lamps and piano lamps, to mention just a few.

Top designers of the day competed to make elaborate ornamental lamps for the luxury market. The luxury lamps and parlour lamps had beautiful shades of cut crystal or, with finely engraved designs, hand-painted opal glass and fluted glass in pretty colours. Some shades were handblown and others had designs in enamel and gold and silver. Still others had beautiful silk shades but these have not survived as the smoke and fumes quickly rotted the material.

The light from oil lamps, fuelled with paraffin, gave a warm friendly glow and a clear easy light to work or read by, and many people, including Queen Victoria, preferred them to all other forms of lighting available.

Simple brass kitchen lamp with central draught burner and globular funnel. £35–£65

Art Nouveau oil lamp in bronze and spelter with Kosmos burner. £150–£275

lampshades

Silk and lace lampshades
for floor and table lamps,
c.1895.

· GLASS · & · · SILK ·

Ordinary oil lamps were used with just a glass chimney and sometimes these were decorated. They would have been used in kitchens and workrooms. Other lamps had a globe which fitted over the chimney and diffused the light. Although called 'globes' they were not necessarily spherical in shape – many looked like an upside-down skirt with a frilled edge. They were often made of coloured, etched and engraved glass.

Most shades and globes, particularly in Victorian times, were made of glass, with the exception of those used on floor-standing lamps which were elaborate creations in silk and lace with glass beads, fringes and tassels. For safety a clear interior glass globe was used inside fabric and card shades. Later on, silk, card and early plastics were often used for shades on oil lamps.

Hanging lamps usually had Vesta or dome-shaped shades in opal white, gold or green glass. Original oil lamp shades are worth collecting, as they had a very high breakage rate. They are not easy to find nowadays. Cranberry and Vaseline glass shades are the most sought after. Engraved and etched shades as well as hand-painted globes transform an ordinary oil lamp into something rather special. A very ordinary brass- or cast iron-based oil lamp with original chimney and no globe would cost from £35 upwards and with an original fancy glass shade about £100–£120, with a vast range of lamps and prices in between. Really elaborately based Victorian oil lamps with Vaseline or cranberry shades could cost £200–£500 and more each, while earlier lamps fetch even more.

using oil lamps

Flat or circular wicks absorb the oil from the reservoir. It is important that they are the right size for their burner. There should be about two inches of wick coiled up in the bottom of the reservoir. When so much of the wick has burnt away that it only just touches the bottom of the reservoir, it must be discarded and replaced by a new one. The wick should be trimmed after every usuage by turning it down so that it is nearly level with the top of the burner and then rubbing away the charred remains with a rag.

When buying oil lamps for practical use, the following needs to be checked:

1 if the reservoir is made of glass, china or pottery there should be no hairline cracks where the oil could leak

2 the burner should be complete and the funnel holder unbroken

3 the wick should wind up and down smoothly

4 the lamp must have a glass funnel of the correct size for the lamp to burn efficiently. An extensive list of different oil lamps manufactured and the correct size funnels is given in an excellent paperback book on oil lamps published by Shire Publications. Some spare parts can be obtained for old oil lamps from Christopher Wrays Lamp Workshop in Kings Road, London. There is no guarantee that they will have the part required, so if anything is missing from a lamp which you want to use, make sure it is a real bargain before buying it or you may find you end up with a totally unusable lamp whose only function will be to look decorative.

5 oil lamps can leave smoke marks on ceilings if placed too close to them. Do not stand them immediately under shelves or cupboards.

Duplex burner oil lamp with flakestone glass reservoir and etched shade, c.1920. £85–£125

using oil lamps

· HOW · TO · · LIGHT ·

Take off the glass shade and chimney. Turn the wick down low and light it with a match or spill. Replace the glass chimney and wait a little while before turning it up again to prevent the glass being cracked by the sudden heat. If the wick is turned too high the flame will smoke and not burn clearly. The glass chimney is there to create a draught and to supply the flame with sufficient air for proper combustion. Chimneyless lamps have a clockwork fan to provide the same function. A tall glass shield or glass bell can be fitted above the chimney to deflect the hot air and to help reduce the blackening of the ceiling above the lamp. Glass or metal bells were frequently used for suspension and harp lamps but they were not suitable for table versions.

Victorian glass oil lamp.

· HOW · TO · · EXTINGUISH ·

With the ordinary lamps the flame should be turned down very low and allowed to go out by itself, or one can blow sharply across the top of the chimney, not down it.

· SAFETY · · LAMPS ·

Some lamps were fitted with a device that automatically extinguished the flame should the lamp be tilted far from vertical or be overturned. Other lamps had levers which automatically raised and lowered the glassware about one to two inches above the burner to make lighting and extinguishing easier, without the necessity of removing the glassware completely.

42

gas

Victorian pottery Dog of Fo gas lamp c.1860
converted to electricity in the 1920s with original
1920s beaded shade. £450+

early history

ABOVE: Brass gasolier for ten rat-tail burners with no shades, c.1814.
BELOW: Floor pedestal gas lamp, c.1814.

The ancient Chinese in the province of Tsee-Leiou-Tsing were the first to experiment with illumination by gas. They are believed to have collected natural gas from 'fire wells' and stored it in animal bladders like large balloons or sausages. When they wanted light they pricked holes in the containers and lit the jets of gas that came forth. 'Fire wells' were bubbling water wells sited over underground coal seams. When a torch was held over them a great flame of fire burst over the water. The torch could be extinguished by dipping it in the water but the main flame continued to burn over the water. It was later discovered that if the water was drawn off, the earth itself could be ignited. This amazing phenomenon was caused by coal gas seeping through the earth and bubbling out through the water.

Thousands of years later 'fire wells' were discovered in South Lancashire in England, and at last the scene was set for the development of the gas industry and gas lighting. Why it took so long for people to discover and exploit gas as an illuminant we shall never know. It is amazing that the Greeks and the Romans with their engineering genius never improved upon the primitive oil lamp, and that the ancient Chinese never exploited the illuminatory powers of natural gas on a greater scale.

Gas lighting, which appears so simple to us now, was a great achievement two centuries ago. The thing that astounded people then was that it was possible to obtain a light *without* a wick. As a Member of Parliament remarked to Richard Murdoch in 1809, 'Ah! my friend, you are trying to prove too much.'

It had been known for a long time that gas could be a very effective form of domestic and municipal lighting. However, the application of this necessitated the installation of gas works and a vast system of pipes to the surrounding streets and buildings for every city and town. The cost of this was prohibitively expensive until the early 1800s.

It took entrepreneurs of great vision and foresight to implement such an ambitious scheme, the scale of which had never been seen before. 'For more than a century gas became the centrally supplied illuminant which lit the cathedral, church and chapel, the palace, shop and private dwelling, the museum, opera house, theatre and concert hall.'

Not only did gas bring light into people's lives but the public bestowed on it amazing health and restorative powers which were not borne out by its effects on household plants except for the aspidistra which seemed to thrive on its close proximity, becoming one of the most popular house plants in Victorian times.

An American promotional brochure issued in Philadelphia *c.* 1850 extolled the virtues of gas light thus: 'The advantage of gas light is manifest. It is much cheaper compared with the light it affords than any other. It saves a deal of time and labour, which would otherwise be expended in filling and trimming lamps, cleaning candlesticks and snuffing candles . . . Gas lights are the very perfection of cleanliness. They can be fixed in any situations, and by means of moveable pipes may be raised, lowered and transferred, according to choice or necessity. The light is agreeable and if properly managed, which management requires no trouble, gives no smoke. In point of cost proportioned to its brilliance it is nearly one-third that of lard burned in our solar lamps, and at least one-sixth that of tallow candles.'

Circular ten-light gasolier for rat-tail burners which burnt like everlasting candles, c.1814.

Leaded cathedral stained glass hall lantern in brass surround, c.1865.
£250–£350

early history

1618   Jean Tardin, a French doctor, produced gas from crushed coal after investigating a 'fire well' near Grenoble.

1659   Thomas Shirley discovered 'burning spring' at Wigan.

c. 1667–91   Rev. J. Clayton conducted coal gas experiments similar to Tardin's.

1726   Dr Stephen Hale distilled coal to make a quantity of gas.

1733   Sir Jas. Lowther experimented with gas at a colliery near Whitehaven.

1764   A Frenchman named Jars had the idea of piping gas from a colliery to the nearby town, but an accidental explosion put paid to its adoption.

1765   Mr Spedding, manager at Lord Lonsdale's colliery near Whitehaven, piped gas to light his own offices. He offered to supply gas to light the streets of Whitehaven but his proposal was refused.

c. 1780   George Dixon used coal gas to illuminate his house in Co. Durham.

1786   Philippe Lebon invented the 'Thermo Lamp'.

1792   Richard Murdoch, a brilliant engineer, distilled gas from coal in iron retorts at Redruth, Cornwall. The gas was forced through a metal tube and lit at the open end. Later he closed the tube to prevent too much gas escaping and pierced holes laterally to make a primitive burner. It is said that this idea was the result of an accidental discovery. In experiments to close the end of the tube he used his wife's thimble which was old and worn with pinprick holes. When it closed the tube, tiny jets of gas came through the holes and could be lighted. Murdoch lit his offices and home

Large wall bracket of a kneeling maiden holding a tray of rat-tail burners above her head, c.1814.

	with piped gas.
1797	Murdoch publicly exhibited gas lighting at Old Cumnock, Ayrshire.
1798	Murdoch lit Boulton and Watt factory in Birmingham.
1801	Lampadeus suggested lighting towns with gas.
1802	Philippe Lebon lit house in Paris with wood gas and coal gas and suggested lighting Paris generally.
1803	Frederick Albert Winsor, a German entrepreneur, illuminated the Lyceum Theatre, London.
1804–6	Boulton and Watt sold their first gas lighting plant to George Lee of Phillips and Lee, a cotton spinning factory at Salford near Manchester. The installation was extended over three years and employed 904 lights comprising 271 Argand and 633 Cockspur burners. These had the illuminant equivalent of 2500 tallow candles. It proved a great economy in running costs. The cost of lighting by candles for one year was £2000–£3000, whereas gas cost only about £600 per annum.
1807	First street lighting. Frederick Winsor lit up Pall Mall as a publicity stunt ostensibly for the King's birthday on 4 June 1807, but in fact as a forerunner to promoting his gas company, the National Light and Heat Company, afterwards called the Gas Light and Coke Company. Winsor claimed without so much as a blush that his coal gas was 'more congenial to the lungs than oxygen!'
1810	Act of Parliament granted a licence to the Gas Light and Coke Company, which remained in business until absorbed by Britain's nationalised gas industry in 1948.
1813	Westminster Bridge first lit by gas.
1816	London generally lit.

Pretty Regency two-light gasolier with glass funnels and decorative scrollwork.

Ruby cut glass bracket with decorative backplate and rat-tail burner, c.1850.

For many years after coal gas was first supplied to the public, it was mainly used for lighting purposes. Even after the introduction of electric lighting (*c.* 1890) the incandescent gas mantle which showed such immense improvement over the old flat flame burner, enabled gas to hold its own as number one illuminant with remarkable success for a very long time.

In the beginning there were very few gas works. In 1822 gas lighting was the business of only four companies but by 1872 it had increased to 18. By 1878 more than eight million tons of coal was being consumed in the United Kingdom for the manufacture of gas. At first there was a restricted gas supply which continued until each house or building had its own gas meter. Usually gas was only available from dusk to 11.30 p.m. and even then the pressure often dropped to unusable levels, resulting in much flickering and faltering of the lamps. It was not until much later in the century, *c.* 1870, when governors were fitted which automatically increased the flow of gas whenever the pressure dropped, that flickering was eliminated.

Brass harp lamp with steel pole and milk glass shade for simple union jet.
£150–£220

· GEORGIAN ·
· & · EARLY ·
· VICTORIAN ·

The earliest gas lights manufactured at the very beginning of the 19th century had all the classical elegance of the Georgian era. There were elaborate gasoliers, wall brackets, floor-standing, newel and pendant fittings for indoors as well as elegant street lights. The fittings were elaborately made in ormolu, bronze, brass or crystal. One design for a gasolier consisted of a circle of birds of paradise perched in a decorative cage, their tails flowing in a scroll-like pattern, their heads pointing upwards with the gas jets coming out of their beaks; another was formed as a corona, the gas jets spurting out from the points of the crown, with cut crystal lustres hanging below to reflect the light. There were great plinths holding vases of flowers with gas jets bursting out of the petals or fronds. Wall brackets were often set with a kneeling classical maiden holding a tray of gas jets above her head or a Greek urn with a single burner. Whilst the fittings were highly decorative the burners themselves were very simple. As the century progressed, hundreds of different burners were experimented with to find the most efficient.

These early gas lights were not designed to have shades of any sort, the gas flame came straight out of the burner and the naked flame burnt like a candle. Different burners could make the flame assume any shape and intensity, but it consumed large amounts of gas for rather poor illumination and gave off a great deal of heat. After the Argand principle was applied to gas burners in 1809, those adapted used simple opaque glass funnels and shades similar to those on oil lamps. Many continued well into the first half of the 19th century to use only the naked flame.

Early Victorian gas pendant with cranberry glass shade. £275–£395

· CHURCH ·
· LIGHTING ·

Churches and chapels are a rich source of antique lighting. Only wealthy people's houses, churches and other public buildings could afford lighting and the Victorian era saw a vast rebuilding and restoration of old churches. Often the clergy opposed the illumination of the London churches by

early history

Decorative brass wall bracket, suspending a large corona of 20 rat-tail burners with crystal lustre drops below, c.1814.

One of a number of Gas Standards of leaves and flowers, providing a vista of light used in Old Boston Church, 1853.

gas. However, in 1853, when the old Boston Church was reopened after extensive restoration and the installation of gas lighting, *The Illustrated London News* enthused: 'The arrangement of the lights is novel and successful. . . . there are rich brass standards [made in the shapes of leaves and flowers] each bearing a considerable number of jets and producing a vista of light. Over the font is suspended a magnificent corona bearing nearly a hundred lights. The adaptation of the modern invention of gas to ancient churches, so as not to destroy the effect of their architectural structure by incongruous fittings, has long been one of the most vexed problems of church restoration . . . [but these] . . . harmonise entirely with the whole building.'

All the lights for this church were designed as if for candles but whereas before there would have been candle cups, they now had gas jets. The gas burnt as an open flame just like a candle. The shape of the flame was determined by the burner used, but it was not designed to carry any sort of shade. It is interesting to see that the very problems we have today when restoring old buildings and houses and also incorporating modern-day amenities, were also seen as problems in Victorian times. It is therefore a great credit to the designers and architects of the time that some of the best lighting fixtures have come from churches. Amazingly, these fixtures look very effective in many domestic and commercial situations today. They blend well in old cottages and barn conversions, and look strikingly effective in large kitchens, dining rooms and family rooms, as well as entrance halls and reception rooms.

gas burners

· THE · RAT · TAIL ·
c. 1806

The earliest burner in widespread use,
it consisted of a single elongated flame
that came from one small hole
perforated in the closed end of a small
metal pipe.

· THE ·
· COCKSPUR ·
c. 1806–8

A burner with three small holes pierced
in the closed end of the tube to give a
triple flame. It gave a light of
approximately one candlepower per
cubic foot of gas consumed per hour.

· THE ·
· COCKSCOMB ·
c. 1806–8

Multiple holes were punched in the
tube of this burner to give a flame in the
shape of a cockerel's comb.

· THE ·
· BATSWING ·
1816

A small pear-shaped steel burner 1/16
inch in diameter with a slit at the top
about 1/40 inch wide.

· THE ·
· FISHTAIL ·
1820

This burner had two gas jets of equal
size, positioned in such a way that,
when alight, they impinged on each
other and produced a fat flame with a
greatly increased light. It was the
forerunner of the very successful union
jet and is believed to have been

invented by James Neilson and James Milne of Glasgow.

· THE · UNION · · JET ·
1880

This burner was developed from the fishtail and improved in 1880. It was provided with an 'economiser' or 'adjustable' burner in 1890. This allowed the burner to give a wider, more even flame and far greater illumination.

· THE · ARGAND · · BURNER ·
1809

Decorative drawing-room lamp with Argand burner and fringed shade manufactured by Sugg, c.1875.

Samuel Clegg, the brilliant young assistant to Richard Murdoch, decided that the Argand burner, which had been used successfully for oil lamps for a number of years, could be adapted for use with gas. It worked on the principle of a circular flame, with air for combustion coming from both the inside and outside of the flame. It usually had a glass chimney similar to those used on oil lamps. This greatly improved combustion, especially when the gas pressure was variable and inadequate which was frequently the case in those times. From 1820, and for the next 60 years, the Argand gas burner was the main alternative to the simple union jet.

· REGENERATIVE · · GAS · LAMPS ·
1853

The principle of regenerative or recuperative lamps, as they were sometimes called, was to preheat the air coming to the gas flame. In this way the candlepower of the lamp could be

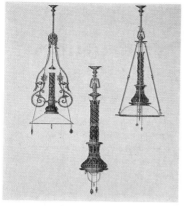

Three inverted recuperative gas pendants with Doulton pottery casings, which were in general use before incandescent lighting was introduced.

increased as much as sevenfold. In 1853 Frankland devised an Argand lamp with a heated air draught that passed between an inner and an outer chimney. Other regenerative burners were developed by Bowditch (1854) and Siemens (1878). They were particularly suitable for shops and public buildings, but tended to look very ugly, being cumbersome and heavy. They do not lend themselves for adaptation in today's homes.

· STEATITE · · BURNERS · & · · GOVERNORS ·

It was generally supposed that five cubic feet of gas gave just as good a light in one burner as in another, until 1858 when William Sugg introduced his burner with a steatite orifice which did not corrode as earlier ones had and did not allow so much heat to escape from the flame. Governors were also fitted to the burners which regulated the flow of gas to them regardless of varying gas pressure. Before governors were fitted, gas consumption would rise as the

gas burners

pressure increased with virtually no improvement in light output. When gas pressure fell, the illumination power could be halved.

· CHRISTIANA · · BURNER ·
1878

In 1874 Sugg introduced his famous 'Christiana' burner which was the best flat flame burner ever made. One of its major improvements was a circular slit to the hollow top steatite head with a regulated opening for the admission of gas. Sugg claimed this burner to be at least 40 per cent superior to the metal top Argand burner and 100 per cent more efficient than an ordinary fishtail burner.

Sugg drawing-room lamp with Christiana burner, c.1875.

· THE · · INCANDESCENT · · MANTLE ·
1885

When electric lighting experiments began to take place in the 1870s the possibility of electric light taking over from gas lighting some time in the future was a real threat to the gas companies. The pressure was then on to improve the light of the simple coal gas flame and make gas the number one illuminant.

Many people started experimenting with substances that could be fitted over the burners and heated to incandescence. Edison, Wenham and Haddon in the United States, Clamond in France, Fahnehjelm in Sweden and Lewis in Britain experimented with various substances but it was Carl Auer Von Welsbach who won the race with his new incandescent gas mantle

Carl Auer von Welsbach's experimental incandescent burner and mantle, 1887.

patented in 1885.

It was not available for sale until 1887 when the Incandescent Gas Light Company was formed, and the design chosen for commercial use was invented by MacTear who was deputy chairman and technical adviser to the Welsbach company. Further developments ensued and a new burner invented by Arthur Heald was adopted in 1890.

The invention of the incandescent mantle, which used less gas than before, yet produced a brighter light, transformed gas lighting, firmly placing it as the number one illuminant and carrying it forward into the 20th century.

The mantles were made of woven or knitted cotton or silk impregnated with chemical salts. After the mantle was saturated in a solution of thorium and cerium, it had to be carefully pressed, dried and shaped into a long cylindrical shape. The fibrous substances were then burnt away, leaving a network of thorium and cerium oxides. In this state the mantle was very fragile. To strengthen it sufficiently to allow transport and handling, it was dipped in a solution of collodion, which had to be burnt off before the mantle was used.

The light was produced by heating the mantle to incandescence by a bunsen burner flame, and not by the illuminatory power of the gas flame itself, as was the case with the flat flame burners. The thorium and cerium oxides glowed white hot when heated and gave a greenish light which was about 12 times as great as that provided by a flat flame burner consuming an equal amount of gas. Even greater increases of candlepower per cubic foot of gas consumed were obtained when inverted and super-heated inverted burners were developed. The

Victorian brass portable table lamp with classical decorations of rams' heads, converted to electricity. £125–£185

gas burners

incandescent burners were at first extremely delicate and fragile, but manufacturing developments quickly followed to improve their strength and durability.

· UPRIGHT ·
· INCANDESCENT ·
· BURNERS ·

The first incandescent burners were upright and varied in detail from manufacturer to manufacturer but the working principle remained the same. The mantle was an elongated 'sausage' shape with a loop at the top which passed over a fork inserted into a small central hole in the burner.

Globes of many shapes, patterns and tints were used to shade the intensified light given off by the mantle, and these were supported by a globe gallery, similar to an oil lamp gallery, which was placed over the chimney gallery or carrier. The burners sometimes had a bypass fitted to turn the bunsen flame on or off.

Upright incandescent burners were frequently used singly or in clusters whenever high illumination was required, such as for display lighting inside and outside shops and also for street lighting. The incandescent burners were cleaned with a small puffer air spray.

The success of the incandescent mantle was amazing: in 1893, 20 000 were sold, but by 1895 the figure had jumped to 300 000. The amount of light obtained also improved rapidly to 20 candlepower per cubic foot of gas in 1889, whereas before only 6–8 candlepower had been normal. The upright mantle did have one drawback – it threw the light upwards, so that the

Edwardian brass portable, converted to electricity, with glass shade.
£95–£150

burner itself produced a shadow at ground level, and if the ceilings were of dark or murky colours much of the available light was lost upwards instead of down at table level where it was needed. Of course all forms of lighting at this time directed the light upwards and several devices were invented to help remedy the problem by making pendant lights adjustable in height.

· THE · INVERTED · · INCANDESCENT · · MANTLE ·

To overcome all these problems a man called Kent produced an inverted incandescent mantle in 1897 which claimed to give 'a downward light free from shadows'. It was only possible to fire the gas flame downwards because the gas supplied to the consumer was now of a better quality and at a more constant and reliable pressure than it had been in the middle of the 19th century. The design of the inverted mantle changed very little over the years except that around 1900, and at least until World War I, the burners were made of brass or copper with porcelain deflectors. During the 1920s and '30s they were gradually superseded by simpler designs in aluminium and magnesia. The aluminium did not

One of a pair of Art Nouveau iron wall lights for inverted mantles, with replacement leaded glass shades, converted to electricity. Pair £195–£285

corrode and remained cleaner than brass. The inverted burners were made in three sizes – full, medium and bijou – providing respectively about 90, 60 and 30 candlepower.

The new inverted incandescent gas burners.

· INVERTED ·
· SUPERHEATER ·
· BURNERS ·

These burners adopted the principle of the earlier recuperative burners and were constructed so that the gas and air were heated immediately before ignition to provide a greater candlepower for each cubic foot of gas burned. Also, two or more small mantles were used in a cluster instead of one larger one. These burners not only gave out more light but also needed less maintenance and had a longer life.

manufacturers

· BRITISH · & · EUROPEAN ·

Ahrendt, Berlin

Bernt and Cervenka, Prague

Boulton and Watts, Soho, Birmingham

W. R. Bowditch

George Bray and Co. Ltd

Julius Bronner of Frankfurt

The Chartered Gas Company which became the Gas Light and Coke Company, London, until it was nationalised into the British Gas Industry in 1948

Clegg

Giroud

G. Hands and Company (trade mark Manu Propria and monogram GH plus three hands)

Hunts Ventilating Gas Lights

Imperial Gas Company

The Incandescent Gas Light Company 1887

S. Leoni of London

Milne, Sons & MacFie of London

New Sunlight Incandescent Co. Ltd, Shoe Lane, London

Peebles

Scholl of London

Schulke

M. Schwartz, Nuremberg

Silcock and Tongue, Aston, Birmingham (specialised in advertising lamps and outside lamps)

South Metropolitan Gas Company

William Sugg Limited

Joseph and James Wadsworth

Welsbach Incandescent Gas Light Co. Ltd of Westminster

Wenham

J. R. Wigham, Dublin

· AMERICAN ·

Archer Pancoast, New York

Archer and Warner

Baker Arnold and Company, Philadelphia

Cornelius and Sons, Philadelphia, 1836 (became Cornelius and Baker 1851)

Henry N. Hooper and Company, Boston

Mitchell Bailey and Company 1854 (became Mitchell, Vance and Company c. 1860)

The Philadelphia Gas Company

Starr, Fellow & Co., New York (became Fellows, Hoffman and Company in 1857)

·LIGHTING·IN·
·THE·USA·

Gas lighting progressed quickly in all
metropolitan areas in the United States
of America although country and
outlying districts continued to use oil
for a very long time, as the introduction
of extensive pipeworks and local gas
works in these areas would have been
uneconomical.

The first chartered gas company in
America was in Baltimore in 1817; this
was followed by another in Boston in
1822, New York in 1823 and New
Orleans in 1835. In 1840 there were
only 11 chartered gas companies in
America, growing to 51 companies by
the end of 1850. After that the industry
expanded very quickly indeed and by
15 June 1863 there were 433 gas
companies in business in the USA with
an additional 23 in Canada. The
majority of the gas companies were
concentrated in the industrialised north-
east. New York alone had 84, whilst
Arkansas had only one. Most of the
companies manufactured coal gas, a few
made 'resin' gas from wood, and only
one, Fredonia in New York, used
natural gas.

At the beginning of the 19th century
most of the gas fittings were imported
from Britain and Europe but as the
century wore on, more and more
companies started to manufacture in
America.

Victorian spelter centurian
portable with flambeau
glass shade, converted to
electricity, c.1875.
£135–£225

outside lights

· STREET ·
· LIGHTING ·

Apart from occasional festival illuminations there is no evidence in England of any attempt at regular street lighting on any large scale until the Middle Ages. In 1415 the mayor of London ordered householders to hang out 'lanthorns' on winter evenings.

From 1694 to 1716 Edward Heming obtained a licence to place lights outside every tenth house from 6 p.m. until midnight from Michaelmas until Lady Day.

In 1736 the City of London took over the task of street lighting and installed 5000 lamps which trebled to 15 000 in two years. Paris had street lighting as early as the 15th century. The Hague in 1618; Amsterdam 1669; Hamburg 1675; and Vienna 1687.

In London, Winsor exhibited a number of gas lights in Pall Mall in 1807. Westminster Bridge was first lit by gas in 1813 and by 1814 most of Westminster was lit. By 1815 the gas system had spread to the West End of London. By 1816 the whole of London generally was lit by gas. In 1823, 215 miles of London streets were lit by 40 000 gas lamps which so delighted everyone that by 1878 these were increased to 55 000.

In 1877 the first electric arc light was erected outside the Gaiety Theatre in London and in 1878 Jablochkoff candles were used to light the Thames Embankment. Although it was possible to light the streets with the brighter light of electricity, gas still had the monopoly for many more years. In fact many smaller towns in England still had gas street lighting well into the 1950s and parts of London are still lit by gas today.

Street lights were made in many

Victorian street lamp in brass and iron with iron bracket, converted to electricity. £325–£450

outside lights

TOP: Panel globe lantern suitable for the exterior of a restaurant, c.1875.

ABOVE: Panel globe outside lantern with eagle and lion's mask decorations in brass, c.1875.

different types, sizes and designs with one or a number of burners fitted into lanterns on brackets or columns of various styles and heights. The illumination varied from 60 candlepower per lamp for suburban roads to as much as 4500 candlepower per lamp for principal thoroughfares in London and provincial cities. At first, street lamps were fitted with upright incandescent mantles but gradually these were superseded by the inverted burners, some using the superheated burners, and one or two burners or clusters varying in numbers of up to 16 of medium size.

Old street lights are much sought after for illuminating old houses and gardens, private driveways, terraces and verandahs. Usually they are converted to electricity, but their original style is so pleasing that no modern lamp can compare with the originals.

When buying old street lamps or other forms of outdoor lighting, always remember that they must be weatherproof and that the electric wires must be fully insulated and protected from any water. The top of the lamp or lantern must be fully enclosed so that the bulb is safe inside the framework of the lamp itself. If the lamps are made of iron they must be protected from rust with a special paint, and brass or copper must likewise be painted or sealed with a protective coat of yacht varnish or similar. The lamps should be checked periodically to make sure they are not rusting. If the lamps are situated some way from the house, special outdoor cable, mineral insulated or armoured PVC sheathed, buried at least 450mm below ground, is required to conform to UK standards.

gas fittings

· BUYING ·
· FITTINGS ·

Most people who buy gaslights today
will want to convert them to electricity.
However, if buying them to use with
gas, check very carefully to make sure
that all the relevant parts are there, that
everything fits neatly and there is no
possibility of gas leakages. It is unlikely
that the burner will be usable and
undamaged, so it must be checked to
see if new burners will fit on to the old
fittings. William Sugg of Crawley,
Sussex, still make original gas fittings
and can supply spare parts, but as there
were so many different manufacturers of
gas fittings and so many different sizes,
it cannot be assumed that modern spare
parts will necessarily fit old fittings.

Old gas fittings can be bought at
auctions, antique fairs and markets or
from specialist antique lighting retailers.
It will be more reliable, although most
expensive, to buy from the latter. The
extra money will be well spent because
the lamps will have been cleaned, safely
adapted to electricity and will more
often than not come complete with a
shade, so that they can literally be taken
home and installed without problems.
Original fittings on sale at auctions or
antique markets are often very tarnished
and corroded, have parts missing and
are not converted to electricity.
Sometimes they will have been polished
up but still not converted, or they may
have wires pushed into them to give
them the appearance of having been
converted. The most common missing
parts are back and ceiling plates. The
gallery that fits above the burner, into
which the shade is screwed, is also likely
to be missing.

Fittings that have an oxidised or
anodised finish, are heavily tarnished, or

Brass pendant gas lamp for
flat-flame burner, with
original milk glass shade,
c.1875. £135–£225

gas fittings

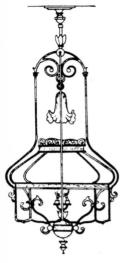

Pendant gas lamp for Argand or flat-flame burner, c.1875.

Art Nouveau brass scotch brackets for upright burners, c.1911. Note the decorative gas taps.

have flaking varnish, will need to be soaked or boiled in a chemical solution to clean them sufficiently for polishing. Old varnish can be removed with paint stripper and fine wire wool which will also remove tarnish. However, it is a very laborious job, and it is hard to obtain the finish of a professional polisher.

Conversion to electricity is not a simple operation. On wall brackets, the aperture near the burner will often be too narrow to take a three-core cable, and the same will be true at the other end, where the key or lever for turning the gas on and off is located. Both these holes will have to be drilled out to make them large enough to take the flex, but the hole must not be too big so as to weaken the fitting or destroy the tap or lever. The burner will have to be replaced with a brass unswitched earthed lampholder, but the screw thread of the pipe may not match the screw thread of the lampholder. On pendant fittings the downrod will end in a large ball-and-socket joint which will be extremely difficult to drill through

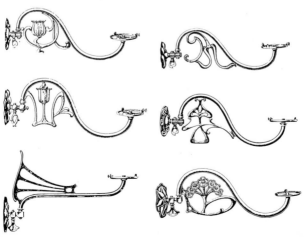

and may have to be taken off completely. A new ceiling plate will then have to be attached in a sufficiently secure way to be able to withstand the weight of the entire light fitting. Where the screw threads of new parts do not match those of the old original ones, the new part will have to be brazed on to the old fitment. However, expensive silver solder must be used, as this cannot be done with the ordinary kind. All metal fitments must be wired with three-core double-insulated cable and earthed to comply with British Standards. They can be earthed at the lampholder or at the backplate. Many other countries do not have the same safety regulations as Britain and do not require their light fittings to be earthed, but often their electricity supply is of a lower voltage.

· TAPS · & · LEVER · COCKS ·

All gas fittings had to have a means of turning the gas supply on and off. Plain brass taps, located either below or above the burner or near the backplate, which screwed on to or into a tube as a permanent fixture, were called 'stop cocks'. Those with a means for disconnecting one part from the other were known as 'union cocks', while those which screwed on to the end of a pipe and had an upward projection at right angles called an 'elbow cock'.

Some wall and pendant fittings had a diagonal crossbar attached above the burner, with a chain hanging down from each side. At the end of the chain there was either a simple split ring, a consumer hook, or a decorative brass tab called a tablet which had the words 'on' and 'off' punched out of the metal, above a ring pull. This fitting was called a 'lever cock'.

Brass pendant gas pole with lever cock, brass tabs and original marbled glass shade, c.1920. £55–£95

ceiling

Brass pendant gas pole
with hand-painted
supastone glass shade,
c.1920. £85–£135

· PENDANTS · & ·
· CHANDELIERS ·

(See also Bowls and Beaded Shades)

A gas lamp that is fitted to the ceiling is
known as a pendant. It could be a
simple pipe that hangs from the ceiling
with one burner, or have a crossbar at
the bottom supporting two burners. If it
had three or more arms, it was called a
gasolier or chandelier.

A simple pendant for a flat flame
burner consisted of a vertical pipe
attached to the ceiling with a ball-and-
socket joint and curved horizontally at
the other end to carry the single burner.
This was often called a rod pendant.
Other early designs for pendants were
based on oil lamp styles such as the harp
lamps, with the gas burners being
substituted for the oil. They either used
a single flat flame burner, a union jet or
an Argand burner. When the
incandescent mantle was introduced
they were frequently adapted to take an
upright mantle.

When the inverted mantles appeared
on the market, pendant lamps really
came into their own. Single rod
pendants with fancy brass decorations
were very popular, as were those fitted

Beaded brass gasolier for
three inverted lights,
converted to electricity,
c.1890. £425–£650

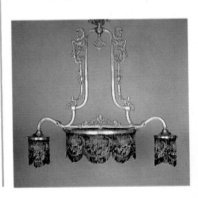

with two swan necks at the bottom of the pole. Fancy brass ornaments were sold separately which could easily be fixed to any plain pendant to convert it to a more ornate fitting. Often pendants had attachments to take chains from which would hang bowls or fancy brass mantles with long beaded silk flounces.

Pendant gas fittings and chandeliers had an irritating habit of vibrating when in use, so several anti-vibration devices were brought out to help remedy the situation. These basically consisted of a spring which was inserted into the down pipe and acted as a buffer to any vibration of the pipes. The weight of the fitting was carried by the spring and the inner tube was protected against corrosion and heat.

Most pendants had ball-and-socket joints at the ceiling connection which was covered with a wooden or metal ceiling plate. These ball-and-socket joints were made of brass, in different sizes and threads. Sometimes the thread in the upper part of the joint did not suit the iron gas barrel and a brass fitting called a 'blushing piece' or a 'diminisher' had to be employed, which screwed internally with threads of different sizes. Commercial brass gas fittings such as brackets and pendants were screwed with a fine thread known as a brass gas thread. Those on iron pipes were coarser and deeper, known as iron gas threads.

When old gas fittings were converted to take the incandescent mantle, frequently a connecting nipple, nose pieces or burner sockets were needed as the new fitments would not screw on to the old.

Continental gasolier in brass, converted to electricity, c.1880.

· BILLIARD ·
· PENDANTS ·

Billiard pendants consisted of a down rod, terminating in a horizontal crossbar which carried three lights for inverted burners. Each light was shaded by a glass coolie-shaped shade; these were in opal, green or amber glass lined with opal. The overall length was *c.* 6ft with a spread of about 7ft 6in. They were made of polished brass or wrought iron and copper and were either very simple or elaborately decorated with brass scrolls, leaves and flowers.

· ADJUSTABLE ·
· PENDANTS ·

The main drawback of pendant gas fittings was that most of the available light was diffused upwards and not directed downwards, where it was most needed. To overcome the problem adjustable pendants and chandeliers were invented. By the 1870s several types of adjustable fitments were in common use.

· WATER-SLIDE ·
· GASOLIER ·

This consisted of a chandelier with three or more arms with burners extending from a central telescopic stem which slid up and down, allowing the arms to be adjusted in height as required for different activities. The telescopic slide contained water which acted as a sealant to prevent unpleasantness from escaping gas. The outer part of the tube was connected to the arms of the chandelier and counterbalanced by a system of three or more weights, chains and pulleys. This

Water-Slide three-light gasolier, used with flat-flame burners. Note the brass pulleys and heavy weights.

became a very popular type of adjustable fitting which was adapted to suit a variety of pendants.

· EXTENSION ·
· CHANDELIERS ·

Extension chandeliers used a more cumbersome and complex system of jointed pipes. They were operated by a spring reel device, whereby the pipes were cantilevered against each other when not in use and held by the spring reel. When this was released the chandelier could be extended to its full length. Some fixtures were adjustable virtually in any direction through the use of universal joints.

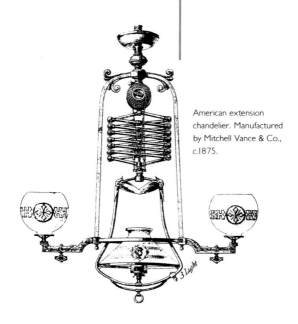

American extension chandelier. Manufactured by Mitchell Vance & Co., c.1875.

· RISE · & · FALL ·
· PENDANTS ·

By the turn of the century, adjustable pendants had become so popular that they continued to be improved. They were adapted for use with the inverted incandescent mantles, even though they already directed the light downwards. The new rise and fall pendants could be drawn down over the centre or moved to the edge of the table for reading. Their construction enabled them to be balanced in any position and to be moved with a touch of the finger. They swung around in a 3ft circle, and measured 3ft 6in from the ceiling plate when up and 7ft 10in when down. Other sizes could be made to order. They were made to rise and fall by two methods. One used a counterweight and consisted of a down rod which terminated with a movable joint holding a crossbar. One end of the crossbar had a movable joint which held another down rod, terminating with an inverted burner and mantle, the other end of the crossbar had a weight which

Rise and Fall rod pendant
with beaded shade, c.1911.

Rise and Fall pendant with
silk shade, c.1911.

Hanwell Rise and Fall pendant in polished brass with silk shade, c.1911.

counterbalanced the lamp on the other side. When the weight was down, the lamp went up and when the weight was pushed vertically to the ceiling the lamp would extend to its full length. The other worked with a spring reel device whereby the gas pipe was contained in a flexible tube which could be coiled into a tight circle when the lamp was not in use and be released by a spring to extend to its full length when required. The latter devices were often called 'Hanwells' after the company that patented the design.

· HALL ·
· PENDANTS ·

Hall pendants were usually single rod pendants with a lantern-type shade fitted over an inverted burner. Earlier hall pendants consisted of leaded glass lanterns, fed by a ceiling fitting, or a lantern surrounded by a harp fitting which fed the gas into the burner which was placed at the bottom of the lantern.

Early Art Deco leaded glass hall lantern. £185–£265

wall

· BRACKETS ·

The simplest gas fittings were wall brackets, never called sconces in the gas era. They were made from a plain brass, copper or iron tube. They came out at right angles from the wall with an upright burner screwed to the end, or they were in the shape of a horizontal 'S' ending in the upward turn which was threaded for the burner. At the opposite end to the burner was a flat backplate for attachment to the wall. A gas tap to turn the gas on and off was located either just below the burner or near the backplate. The brass backplate was usually screwed on to a larger turned wood plate which hid the connections and was fixed neatly to the wall.

The brass pipes were either plain or decorated with simple repetitive patterns, such as a twist or small circles engraved on them. The backplates and gas taps were often quite decorative, and were made in attractive shapes.

Brackets that were fixed in one position were called 'stiff' but frequently they were made to swivel from side to side. The plain horizontal brackets often had one to three joints, so that they could be extended to 33 inches, and each joint allowed the bracket to be swivelled from side to side. When the arms were folded back on themselves

One of a pair of brass brackets with original glass globes, c.1870.
Pair £350–£475

Art Nouveau brass bracket with cranberry glass shade, c.1911. £125–£195

the lamp would only extend about 12 inches from the wall. Sometimes a large pendant lamp or small chandelier was attached to one of these extending wall brackets instead of being suspended from the ceiling. Presumably this was to minimise the pipe-work and make installation easier, but it also meant the lamp could extend over the table when needed.

Other wall brackets closely resembled candle sconces and fitted fairly closely against the wall. They had one or two upward-pointing arms, fitted with upright incandescent candle mantles with glass galleries which were shaded with silk or parchment candle shades. They looked attractive but did not emit a great deal of light.

· SWAN · NECK ·

One of the most popular wall brackets was a brass or copper tube bent into the shape of an 'S' or a swan's neck. Until the invention of the inverted incandescent mantle, the 'S' was a horizontal one with an upturned end for the burner. After that time it took the natural shape of a swan's neck and the incandescent mantle was attached to the down-pointing gallery so that a shade could be attached. The gallery consisted of a circular attachment in brass, copper or later aluminium. It either had two

One of a pair of Art
Nouveau brass swan
necks with original glass
shade, c.1920.
Pair £175–£250

upturned wings to allow air to the
burner or an upturned fan on one side
of the gallery. Often the galleries were
lined with porcelain reflectors.

Frequently these swan neck wall
lights were embellished with brass
ornaments. Art Nouveau designs
consisted of leaves and flowers entwined
around the stem with the shade like a
flower bud emerging. Sometimes the
entire bracket was made in the shape of
an animal, or of a lady holding the shade
in her hands. Although the most
common swan necks were single light
brackets, those with two or three arms
were also made. They are worth looking
for as they are especially useful today in
places where extra light is required,
while still keeping a period look.

Plain brass swan neck with
original glass shade, c.1911.
£55–£75

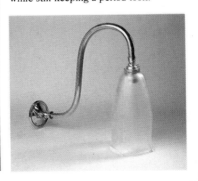

Gas brackets were also made in cut glass, porcelain and pottery with the metal tube running through the centre of the glass or china, but they are not seen very often.

Pair of brass bijoux swan necks with mica shades.
Pair £145–£195

· BIJOU ·

Bijou gas brackets were made for use with small inverted gas mantles and they gave about 30 candlepower. They were very tiny swan neck brackets with delightfully pretty miniature glass shades about 1⅞ inches wide and 2 or 3 inches in length. Converted to electricity they take about a 25-watt bulb. They look very attractive in cottages or in corridors, cloakrooms, niches or bedrooms and are the ideal answer when a very low-level background light is required.

newels

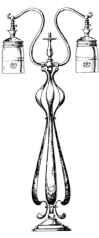

Art Nouveau brass two-light newel, c.1911.

Immovable upright fittings with a burner at the top and a fixing plate at the bottom were generally termed 'newel' standards. They were intended for fixing to desks, pulpits, tables or to the newel posts at the bottom of stairs. They were also screwed to shop counters, hotel desks, restaurant tables and bars. They varied in height from about 30 inches to 48 inches, excluding shades. They were often made in pairs to go either side of the stairs, each end of a desk or on plinths on each side of a doorway or entrance.

Originally constructed to take single burners, they were also made with arms to take two or more lamps. Newels were adapted to use the new inverted incandescent mantles – the centre pole was curved out slightly at the side and then swung over so that the burner hung downwards. Double newels had a swan neck on either side of the upright rod, with both burners pointing down. The newels for inverted burners were either plain brass with businesslike coolie shades or decorative flowing Art Nouveau designs with pretty flowerlike glass shades.

The early newels were very grand and solid fixtures, often made like tall plinths or obelisks or in the shape of a person holding a light or group of lamps above its head.

Single and double Edwardian brass newel lamps.

· STANDARDS ·

Newel fittings were really types of 'standard', but true standards were floor-standing fixed lamps. They could be fairly simple to amazingly elaborate figures standing 85 inches high. The figures for gas mostly supported a large single burner but some could support as many as five burners. Like the newels, they were often made in pairs. Very early standards (*c.* 1806) depicted figures or columns supporting a corona of unshaded burners which looked rather like large floor-standing candelabras. Standards in mid-Victorian times often copied the designs of lampposts and had one, three or five arms with burners. They were used mainly in grand public buildings.

By the end of the 19th century there were gas standards of similar design to those used for oil, suitable for domestic situations. By the 1930s portable standards were being made which looked very similar to the standard lamps of today except that they used gas fed into the fittings by a flexible rubber tube. Gas standards were usually made of brass, bronze or iron and copper but in the 1930s they also ran metal gas pipes inside wooden lamps.

Floor-standing pillar lamp, c.1814.

table

Engraved brass portable,
c.1920 converted to
electricity. £125–£195

BELOW RIGHT: Art
Nouveau brass portable
with painted shade, c.1910.
£135–£225

BELOW: One of a pair of
fine spelter portables with
painted glass shade.
Converted to electricity,
c.1875. Pair £450–£650

· PORTABLES ·

Portables were table or desk lamps that
received their gas by way of flexible
rubber hose, similar to those used on
bunsen burners in school laboratories,
connected to an outlet on a nearby wall.
Portables were frequently made in the
shape of classical figures holding the
burner and shade high above their
heads. Children, cupids, soldiers and
animals were popular subjects. They
were made in plain and decorative
columns, vases and obelisks. They often
incorporated a cigar lighter as well as a
light. The ever-popular Student's Lamp
and Queen's Reading Lamp were also
made as gas portables, complete with
adjustable column. The portables
ranged in height from about 10 to 18
inches excluding the shade. They were
usually fairly heavy to prevent them
being overturned and always had
upright burners.

The earliest burners had no shades at
all and were like everlasting candles.
Open-ended globes with galleries that
fitted under the burners were then
used. Later, silk and parchment shades
became popular, but the burners had to
be protected with glass or mica
cylinders. Gas portables continued to be
made until World War II.

lampshades

The earliest shades used on gas fittings had small-diameter bases, and the shapes and styles were very similar to those used on oil lamps. Wide-based shades were not made until 1875 when it was found that the wider bases provided an even flow of air to the burners and so greatly reduced flickering. These wide-necked shades were so successful that they largely supplanted the small-based variety for flat flame burners.

Shades in the 1870s and '80s were usually large and globular in appearance with a slice taken off the top where the globe was open to the ceiling. Some were made quite clear with a ripple in the glass, others were frosted, half frosted or half milk glass and half clear. Ornamentation was added by frosting (acid etching), etching using stencils, or by cutting a design into the glass. Etching was deep or shallow, depending on how long the acid was left in contact with the glass. Often the bolder pattern was cut and the more intricate designs were etched. Some shades were tinted

A selection of gas globes, c.1875.

lampshades

Glass globes, c.1911.

or had colour at the edges only. Others were elaborately hand painted with beautiful pictures of flowers and birds and other designs.

After the 1880s the shades were made in a vast variety of shapes, often like sugar bowls or basins with scalloped or crimped edges. Some had thin wavy lines etched around the edges in close parallels and were often tinted pink – this was called threaded ruby.

When the incandescent mantles were introduced, fireproof glass chimneys were used, and some of these had an additional opaline shade with a frilly edge that sat over the chimney. Others had crystal and etched upright globes that sat on a gallery and extended over the chimney. Extra-wide globes, plain and decorated, were used for lamps with cluster burners. Outside globes were protected by wire cages that fitted over the glassware.

Special shades were needed for the inverted incandescent burners and these came in all sizes to fit the many different burners available. Now that the shades hung downwards, they were frequently made in bell and flower

Silk handkerchief shade used for pendant gas lights, c.1925.

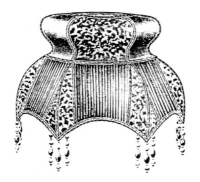

shapes. The tulip shape was particularly attractive – sometimes made to look like a slightly open bud, at other times left more open with crimped edges. They were frequently acid etched or crystal etched and, if coloured, rose, green and citron were the usual hues. Sometimes the colour was shaded or introduced at the edges only. For the bijou burners there were exquisite tiny shades with apertures of 1 inch or 2½ inches, in straw opalescent, clear optic or crystal etched and many other fancy designs and finishes.

Gas shades were also made in all the types of glass used for oil and electric light fittings such as cranberry, opaline and Vaseline. (See also Index.)

· ALBATRINE ·

In 1875 William Sugg offered a vast range of beautiful albatrine glass globes, rounded in shape but open at the top with a smaller opening at the bottom, which fitted into galleries on their Christiana burners. These shades, in pretty opaque opal-coloured glass, were very similar to oil lamp shades of the time, and were exquisitely hand painted by talented French artists. The designs

lampshades

in wonderful soft colours ranged from children, flowers, trees, birds and animals to peaceful countryside and fishing scenes. When lit the pictures seemed to come to life.

· SILICA ·

Standard plain shades were made of unbreakable heat-resistant silica for use with wall brackets. They had a slightly streaked white appearance and gave a pleasantly milky glow when lit. Silica shades looked like glass. They were not decorated with etched or painted designs but left completely plain. Often fairly tubular in shape with a flange or crimped edge at the bottom, these shades were also called 'Vitreosil' or mica.

A selection of glass globes for bijou burners, c.1911.

· SUPASTONE ·

A popular glass for inverted burner
shades was 'supastone'. This was an
opaque creamy-white three-ply glass,
consisting of a centre of opal glass with
clear flint on the inside and polished
satin matted on the outside. This gave
an intense white light of glareless
reflection which was restful on the eyes.
It was considered the most perfect type
of glassware for ornamental appearance
and had smooth internal and external
surfaces which were easy to clean.
Supastone was either moulded into
attractive self-patterns or carefully hand
painted with pretty floral scenes and
other motifs by specialist artists. It was
extensively used in shops, hotels,
offices, theatres, public buildings as well
as for domestic lighting.

· REFLECTORS ·

The need to maximise the available
light was especially urgent for shop and
sign displays and for desk and working
lamps, so reflector shades were used.
These ranged from simple coolie or
pudding-basin shapes in iron with white
enamelled interiors, or green or amber
glass lined white, to double glass shades
with the inner part made of silvered
glass.

· HOLOPHANE, ·
· STILETTO ·
· PRISM ·
· SHADES ·

These reeded glass shades, in a variety
of shapes and sizes, are usually made of
clear glass but they can be tinted. The
glass is moulded into refractive prisms
which reflect the light. There are three

lampshades

Prismatic crystal shade.

main types: 'intensive' for general
illumination; 'extensive' for lateral
illumination; and 'focusing' for
concentrated illumination. On the inside
rim, the trademark 'Holophane' and
often a registered number were
moulded into the glass. Holophane is
the name of the man who invented this
type of glass.

· BOWLS · FOR ·
· CENTRE ·
· PENDANTS ·

Bowls on chains were attached to the
central down rod of single pendant gas
lights and these prevented glare and
diffused the light upwards to give
background light for the whole room.
They were only really effective in rooms
where the ceilings and walls were
painted white or a pale colour which
would reflect the light.

Early bowls were dish-shaped and
made of alabaster or milk glass. Later
'supastone' glass was used. Designs and
patterns were either hand painted on
them or transfer printed. Some bowls
were simply acid etched to give a

frosted appearance, or cut with intricate designs like the smaller shades. The bowls ranged from 8 to 16 inches in diameter. In the 1930s bowls made of flakestone glass were cheap and became very popular. They were of marbled appearance and were sold in many colours. They are popular again today with young people setting up home.

· BEADED ·
· SHADES ·

In the 1920s beads of every description were very fashionable and they were used extensively to make stunning evening and dance dresses like the wonderful fringed creations the flapper girls wore. As always, interior decoration tended to follow in the footsteps of women's *haute couture*, and so beads began to be introduced for objects for the home. Painted glass shades trimmed with pretty 3- or 4-inch glass bead fringing became popular and looked very decorative on single-stem gas pendants. Smaller beaded shades were used on swan-neck scroll brackets and for shading the light on two- or three-arm inverted pendants. Sometimes very

Brass three-light gasolier with central lever cock and beaded glass shades, c.1920. £325–£450

lampshades

tiny beads were used which made up an intricate pattern of flowers, birds, garlands and bows, which sparkled in the sunlight as well as when illuminated at night. At other times large and small beads were mixed to form pleasing patterns. Beaded shades are very much in demand today and fetch very high prices. When buying the original beading, the beads will almost certainly have to be rethreaded, as the original thread becomes weak with age. Rethreading is not a difficult job but special beading needles and strong thread are needed and it is extremely time-consuming.

Some pendant lights had a 9- or 10-inch diameter brass ring, about 2 or 3 inches wide, which was suspended from the gas pole. A silk flounce was threaded on to a piece of wire which fitted inside the brass band. The flounce was weighted with a 2-inch beaded fringe. Alternatively, larger beads were sewn around the edge at about 2-inch intervals to look like tassels. Sometimes the flounce was made up entirely of beads, and at other times the silk material was overlaid with lace ribbons, garlands and artificial flowers.

Victorian and Edwardian silk shades for gas lamps were very elaborate, reminding one of the hats and dresses of the period. Shades grew much simpler after World War I, but were still frequently trimmed with beads or bead fringing. Occasionally 6- or 8-inch silk fringing was used instead of beads, presumably for economy. It still looked very effective but as it was not weighted and was quite flimsy it would move with any draught or breeze.

Silk and beaded flounces for gas pendants were very popular in this country and are having quite a revival

Victorian beaded gas pendant for flat-flame burner, originally made to slide, but now missing weights. Corona decorated with lion's mask, c.1875. £295–£355

Large square mahogany and amber crackle glass shade with long silk fringe for pendant gas pole.
£95–£150

today. The flounces can be made to suit the rest of the furnishings in the room, and when lit they give a pleasant pool of light over a table. Many were intended for use on Rise and Fall pendants and look most attractive over a dining table. All British catalogues of the Victorian era feature these shades extensively, whereas very few show any with the leaded glass Tiffany-style shades so typically American, which are so frequently labelled Victorian or Edwardian today. The French did have some pretty silk and beaded shades but they seemed to concentrate more on producing beautiful glassware, either blown and moulded in wonderful colours or exquisitely hand painted or enamelled.

Whenever beaded or silk shades were used on gas lamps the burners had to be protected with simple fireproof globes or cylinders. These protectors were made of glass or mica.

In the 1920s and '30s mock vellum, parchment and early forms of plastic were used for lampshades, both for pendants and table lamps. The shades were usually made in panels, stitched together with cord or ribbon and always attractively trimmed with silk or bead fringing or tassels. Wooden beads and

lampshades

also the new moulded plastic beads were often used instead of glass, as they were much cheaper. These shades, like the silk and beaded ones, could only be used on gas lights with protectors.

· SMOKE · BELLS ·

To protect ceilings and furnishings from fumes and smoke damage, many pendant light fittings incorporated a smoke bell, top or ceiling shade. The smoke bells were usually made of brass or iron, although some were made of glass. The shape was frequently a very open bell with crimped or fluted edges, often as large as 4 inches in diameter, but smoke bells were also made in the shape of shells or a saddle. These are not seen very often nowadays and are well worth collecting.

Ceiling shades were much bigger, in sizes from 6 to 18 inches diameter and looked more like upside-down soup plates, with a ring on the bottom. They were made of enamelled steel or iron and also helped to disperse the heat back into the room. Glass ones were called ceiling smoke consumers.

Upright incandescent mantles, protected by mica glass chimneys, could be fitted with a variety of smoke tops. In porcelain, aluminium or brass they were cone or crown-shaped and clipped on to the chimney with one or two clips or a circular gallery. They never completely covered the top but had a hole in the centre, at the sides of a pierced pattern, to allow the by-products of combustion to escape.

Many fittings had china or enamel deflectors which fitted above the burners and inside the gallery. These were like a pair of wings: they helped to deflect the heat and light away from the burner.

electric

Enamelled brass lamp base in the shape of a Japanese
lady holding a pearl, c.1910. £95–£195

All sources of light before the discovery of electricity gave very little concentrated light. The incandescent gas mantle certainly rectified this, but it was not marketed until the 1880s when the first electric filament lamps were also just becoming available.

· THE · ARC ·
· LAMP ·
1808

The possibilities of using electricity to produce light had been realised as early as 1808 when Sir Humphrey Davy demonstrated his carbon arc lamp at the Royal Institute in London. This consisted of two pencils of carbon placed a little apart. When an electrical current was passed through them, an arc of light jumped across the gap between the pencils to complete the circuit. The light produced was extremely brilliant and shone too brightly to be useful domestically but it was excellent for illuminating large outdoor areas.

Art Nouveau spelter table lamp.

The development of electric arc lamps continued in the 1840s with demonstrations in the streets of Paris. These were so successful that by 1878 20 areas of Paris were lit by electricity, as were the principal places in Brussels, Madrid and St Petersburg (Leningrad). The Parisians loved the new lamps and a newspaper report of 1878 describes the illuminations for the Paris fête: 'The Place de la Concorde was transformed into a fairy palace . . . The fountains sent forth their sparkling streams, while coloured electric lights came pouring down on the whole square from under the trees of the Tuilleries Garden . . .'

Electricity cost far more than gas but because of its brightness fewer lamps were needed. In Paris, 201 gas lamps were replaced with just 16 electric

lights, which provided a 30 per cent
saving but gave three and a half times as
much light.

· THE ·
· JABLOCHKOFF ·
· 'CANDLE' ·
c. 1876–7

A very simple arc lamp, invented by the
Russian Paul Jablochkoff was used for
several years for street lighting. Its
disadvantage was that the 'candles'
needed replacing frequently.
Jablochkoff 'candles' were used to light
the Victorian Embankment near
Westminster Bridge in 1878. The arc
lamps were excellent for street and
outdoor display lighting but far too
brilliant for practical use in the home or
factory.

Victorian spelter man on
an eagle table lamp with
original flame shade,
c.1895. £155–£225

· THE ·
· INCANDESCENT ·
· FILAMENT ·
· BULB ·

The key to successful electric lighting
was to be the incandescent filament
bulb, which had been the subject of
much research since the 1840s. Edward
Staite demonstrated the theory in 1845
with a glass bulb which was pierced
with two platinum wires supporting a
carbon filament between them. When
an electric current was passed through
the system, the filament became
incredibly hot and glowed
(incandesced). However, for it to be
really successful the bulb needed to be
hermetically sealed, which was not
possible until 1865 when the German
Hermann Sprengel invented the
mercury vacuum pump. In an unsealed
bulb the filament reacted with the

Victorian spelter cherub
lamp with original
flambeau shade.
£150–£225

residual air in the glass and became carbonised which caused gradual disintegration of the filament itself and blackened the inside of the bulb with carbon particles.

The remaining problem involved finding the best size, shape, thickness and material which would produce the most durable filament with the highest incandescence. Several people were involved in independent research to find the solution.

· EDISON ·
· & · SWAN ·

History awards the honour of inventing the incandescent filament bulb in 1879 to Thomas Alva Edison, an American. However, he was not really the first, neither was Sir Joseph Swan who demonstrated his lamp a year earlier in 1878. Several other people, including Sir Hiram Maxim, St George Lane-Fox and William Sawyer, had also successfully demonstrated incandescent filament lamps. What Edison had achieved was the first practical commercial lamp which, when lit on 20 October 1879, had glowed continuously for 40 hours. Swan's lamp had lasted only about two hours and the others had produced lamps which flickered and glowed briefly before expiring.

Swan had established his own company, the Swan Electric Lamp Co. Ltd, in 1878/9 and he worked closely with R. E. B. Crompton who had set up a business in *c.* 1877 importing lamps and generators from Paris. By 1879 Crompton had his own manufacturing plant in Chelmsford and it was Crompton who installed the 1000 Swan lamps at the Savoy Theatre in 1881. The new Swan lamps, with their small size and steady light needing no

One of a pair of silver-plated brass hunting horn and bow and tassle wall lights by Ediswan, *c.*1895. Pair £350–£550

attention from the user, speedily secured an expanding luxury market.

For several years there was much acrimonious conflict between Edison and Swan with litigation about patents and who was first. They finally managed to resolve their differences by co-operating in a commercial venture, the Edison and Swan United Electric Company Ltd, which they set up in England in 1883. Hiram Maxim and St George Lane-Fox also entered into commercial production of their lamps.

Cut crystal Art Nouveau ceiling light with brass gallery, c.1907. £95–£175

· PRINCIPAL ·
· EVENTS ·

1808 Invention of arc lamp by Sir Humphrey Davy.

1840 Grove and de Moleyns made experimental platinum wire lamps.

1845 Edward Staite demonstrated the theory behind the incandescent filament bulb.
Starr and King suggested that an electric lamp could be made using metal or carbon filaments in a vacuum.

1865 Hermann Sprengel invented the mercury vacuum pump.

1873 Lodiguine made an experimental carbon filament nitrogen-filled lamp.

c. 1877 The British electric lighting industry began when R. E. B. Crompton imported Serrin lamps and Gramme generators from Paris.

1877 Six arc lights installed outside Gaiety Theatre in London.

1878 Sir Joseph Swan, who had been researching electric light since 1848, first demonstrated his incandescent filament bulb which burned for about two hours.
Twenty areas of Paris now lit by electricity, also principal places in Brussels, Madrid and St Petersburg.

1879 Thomas Alva Edison, an American from Menlo Park, New York, successfully

Bronze Hall Lantern with original glass, c.1895. £300–£500

demonstrated the first practical model of a commercially viable incandescent electric lamp which glowed for 40 hours.

Blackpool illuminations commenced with arc lamps.

1880 First domestic dwelling lit by Swan's electric lamps was that of Sir William Armstrong at Craigside near Newcastle. Later that year Swan installed an electric lighting system in his own home in Gateshead.

1881 Royal Exchange and Mansion House lit by Siemens arc lights.

Jablochkoff lights used to light Victoria Embankment.

Billingsgate Fish Market lit by arc lights. June: The House of Commons lit by incandescent filament electric lamps.

December: Crompton installed 1000 Swan lamps at the D'Oyly Carte Savoy Theatre in London.

First public electric generating supply system started at Godalming, Surrey.

1881 First International Electrical Exhibition where Swan, Edison, St George Lane-Fox and Sir Hiram Maxim showed their incandescent electric lamps.

1882 Thomas Edison established an electricity supply station for New York.

First public supply of electricity in London was the Holborn Viaduct station set up by Thomas Edison in January 1882.

Robert Hammond set up an electricity supply station in Brighton.

1883 Edison and Swan resolved their differences by co-operating in a commercial venture in England, the Edison and Swan United Electric Co. Limited, with a trade name of Ediswan, seen on many early lamps and fittings.

1883 Sir Coutts Lindsay lights his Grosvenor Gallery in New Bond Street with incandescent electric lamps, which was so amazingly successful that in answer

Edwardian wrought iron library lamp with original bent art glass petal shade. £185–£500

to public demand he installed additional generators under his gallery to supply power for electric lighting to surrounding dwellings, shops and institutions.

c. 1883 Sebastian Ziani de Ferranti was already in business on his own account, manufacturing alternators, arc lamps, meters and other electrical equipment.

1886 Ferranti became Engineer-in-Chief of the Grosvenor Gallery generating station, which now supplied the power for 26 000 lamps.

1887 London Electricity Supply Corporation (LESCO) founded, later to become the London Electricity Board (LEB).

1889 Deptford power station opened.

1893 Jandus arc lamp invented, the first really successful closed arc lamp.

1897 'Flame' arc lamp developed.

c. 1904 From the turn of the century electric trams were introduced (until that time electricity had been supplied almost entirely for lighting purposes which had not been very economical, as costly generators had been left idle for much of the time).

1909 Electrification of suburban train services.

1914–18 World War I.

1915 Over half a million homes in UK now wired to receive electricity.

1920 Nine independent companies, together with LESCO, formed the London Power Company (LPC).

1920s All-in domestic tariff introduced; one halfpenny per unit (less than one-quarter of a new penny) plus a fixed charge based on number and sizes of rooms. Electricity companies provided a scheme for house wiring whereby consumers could pay on weekly terms, and also supplies for the Fixed Price Light Company which enabled people in poorer areas to pay a fixed charge of sixpence (2½p) per lamp per week. All electrical appliances could be hired

One of a set of two two-arm and one three-arm Victorian ormolu Louis XIV style wall lights. Set £400–£600

Set of three Art Nouveau copper water lily wall lights made for Harrods, c.1901. Set £125–£195

	for a small weekly sum.
1924	Trial scheme for lighting whole of Deptford by electricity (97 per cent), not just street lighting but electricity for every house.
1931	Still less than half the homes in Britain had electric light.
1930s	Standardisation of frequencies, currents and voltages was the preoccupation of an industry that had developed in such a haphazard way.
1935	National grid in full operation.
1939	Nearly 75 per cent of homes in Britain now wired for electric light.
1939–45	World War II.
1948	Nationalisation of electricity industry.

· SUPPLY ·
· STATIONS ·

Just as gas lighting could not be developed without a network of gasworks and pipe systems, so electric lighting could not have grown into the successful industry it is today without electricity generating stations and a network of cables. Yet the first electricity supply station was founded only just over 100 years ago in 1887, in Goldalming. This was followed by other small generating stations supplying only customers in their immediate vicinity.

A big breakthrough was the opening of Deptford Power Station in 1889 to supply a large proportion of London customers. In the main the industry progressed in a very haphazard and unco-ordinated way. Public supplies were mainly restricted to the large cities but individuals could purchase their own generators just big enough to run a small household lighting system. Harrods featured many such generators in their catalogues from 1900 to 1930.

By 1915 just over half a million homes were wired for electric light. This was only a very small proportion of the population, and gas continued to feature widely as the number one illuminant. Oil lamps were still used extensively in country areas where there was no supply of gas.

After World War I it was decided that if the electricity industry continued to expand, then it must be standardised. There were so many independent companies, operating throughout the country that lights and appliances used in one area could not be used in another. London alone had 50 different systems of electrical supply with 24

French Art Nouveau lace lantern made by first dipping the lace in a strong sugar solution. The crystallised lace is then dipped in molten metal and cooled. £125–£165

Canadian bronzed cast iron five-arm chandelier with replica leaded glass shades, c.1912. £275–£350

different voltages and 10 different frequencies provided by jealously independent power companies and local authorities.

It was also in the 1920s that different schemes appeared to encourage more and more people to use electricity, and there were incentives to housebuilders to electrify all new housing. So, although in 1931 less than half the homes in Britain had electricity, by 1939 nearly 75 per cent of all homes were wired up to receive some electrical supply. At last electricity had overtaken gas as the number one illuminant, but it is sobering to think that, whereas electricity has maintained its prominent position for over 50 years now, gas was the prime illuminant for over 100 years.

In the 1880s and '90s electricity was still a great novelty. *The Times* enthused: 'The light is quite as easy to manage as gas, while the softness, the purity and the agreeableness are such that a return to any other method of illumination would now be out of the question. The pictures, books, and decorations have no chance of injury; the ceilings and walls remain unspoiled, while the difference in health felt after sitting for an evening in a room electrically illuminated, and another lit by gas, must be experienced before it can be appreciated.' (And yet gas companies were saying once how marvellously healthy gas light was!)

Edison and Swan designed and manufactured a wide range of light fittings between 1883 and 1900, varying in illumination from 1 to 1000 candlepower. The most popular lamp was about 16cp, which is roughly comparable to the modern 25-watt bulb.

Swan's glass bulbs were blown for him by Stearn while Edison's were blown by Boehm. Light bulbs were extremely costly and could be made in

One of a pair of gilded gesso cherubs holding a crystal lustre lamp in each hand, c.1920.
Pair £500–£650

almost any shape or size. They were even supplied in cut glass or engraved with a pattern. For designers the electric light bulb was an amazing opportunity for creative designs. The main drawbacks were that the bulb was often thought to be too bright, and it was such a novelty that in the beginning there was no attempt to conceal it as we do today. Also, early bulbs only lasted about 400 hours, as against 750–1000 hours for modern ones.

As electricity slowly began to assert itself over other forms of domestic lighting, there was much competition between the manufacturers to produce brighter but less dazzling bulbs. Other illuminants for the bulbs were discovered which complemented rather than challenged the popularity of the standard bulb. They were: osmium (1897), tantalum (1905), tungsten (1907), neon (1922), mercury (1932) and fluorescent tubes (1940).

Although electric light fittings were being manufactured and installed from 1881, they were not readily available and even leading stores like Harrods did not include them in their catalogue until 1895. The first electrical fittings closely followed the patterns of those for gas. However, soon artists and designers were inspired by the magic and immediacy of the new lighting system with its brightness and flexibility to produce more imaginative designs.

Three-tier crystal chandelier with painted iron leaves and china roses entwined up the stem, c.1920. This chandelier would look lovely in a conservatory. £395–£595

styles 1890–1928

Victorian ormolu table
lamp with crystal drops
and painted shade.
£150–£225

Victorian brass table lamp
decorated with garlands
and swags with matching
painted shade. £125–£195

· VICTORIAN ·

The general style at the end of the last
century was very elaborate and tending
to rather ponderous and intricate
designs. Victorian electric light fittings
were produced in very similar styles to
those used for gas and oil. In fact,
catalogues of the period show designs
for floor-standing lamps with a note
saying they could be supplied either for
oil or wired for electricity. Rococo and
neo-classical styles were still popular and
the general look was eclectic and very
decorative. Victorian styles continued to
be made well into the Edwardian era.

The light bulb itself was such a
novelty that very little thought was
given to concealing it and it frequently
appeared as the stamen of a flower or
even just the naked bulb in all its glory.
Bulbs could be ordered in all shapes and
sizes and could even be engraved,
although it soon became apparent that,
as the life of the bulb was relatively
short, it was not economical to go to
great lengths to decorate it.

· ARTS · & · CRAFTS · · MOVEMENT ·

The Arts and Crafts revolutionary
movement started around the middle of
the 19th century and was led in
England by William Morris and C. R.
Ashbee and by Frank Lloyd Wright in
the United States. Although the artists,
architects, designers and craftsmen who
belonged to and were inspired by the
movement had widely differing
viewpoints, they all agreed on the
central principle that a well-designed
environment, filled with soundly
constructed and well-designed
buildings, objects and articles, could
only enhance and improve the fabric of
modern society for producers and

Arts and Crafts copper chandelier with Vaseline glass shades.

consumers alike. It was basically a movement that celebrated the skills of the craftsman as a designer and the designer as a craftsman, and its influence was felt on both sides of the Atlantic. Creative craft work was seen as a joyous occupation that men and women could participate in with total equality.

The style of furniture and light fittings was essentially simple and aesthetically pleasing, yet practical and well made. It lacked ostentation and contained an air of gracefulness.

· THE ·
· SHAKERS ·

The traditions of home-spun values, rediscovered by the pioneers of the Arts and Crafts movement, had been nurtured by the Quakers for more than a century. The Quakers who left England in the 17th century to escape persecution, settled in America and became known as Shakers. They continued to uphold the same values and principles in their new homeland and the style of their furniture, architecture and associated objects, including light fittings, has become very popular. Simply made, soundly constructed and without excessive decoration, items rely on clean, simple and practical lines for their charm.

· ART ·
· NOUVEAU ·

Art Nouveau was a development of the Arts and Crafts movement which progressed alongside it at the end of the 19th and beginning of the 20th century. It was a reaction against the rather heavy, cluttered style so popular in Victorian times. Art Nouveau was obsessed with totally integrated interiors and with all aspects of a building and its interior existing in harmonious unity. This led many architects and artists to design light fittings as part of the whole unified interior.

Art Nouveau is full of movement, wonderful flowing whiplash curves, entwined leaves and flowers, berries and buds and women with flowing hair and billowing robes. Art Nouveau designers drew their inspiration from the whole spectrum of nature but botanical and entomological motifs were especially popular, in particular the dragonfly,

BELOW, LEFT TO RIGHT:
French painted iron dragon breathing not fire, but a bunch of red roses from his mouth. Silk shade. £295+

Art Nouveau brass table lamp with original shade painted with parrots. £195–£300

French Art Nouveau iron heron lamp with pâte-de-verre shade. £220–£350

art nouveau

French Art Nouveau chandelier with wrought iron roses and mounts housing pâte-de-verre centre bowl and three bell shades. £225–£485

Art Nouveau five-arm brass chandelier with opaline glass shades.

BELOW, LEFT AND RIGHT:
Seated Art Nouveau lady in gilded spelter holding flower, shade missing. £175–£250

Art Nouveau bronze lady holding lamp above her head and small child peeping around her skirt. £175–£295

Art Nouveau two-arm gilded iron wall sconce. £225–£295

One of a pair of bronze Art Nouveau wall lights with cut crystal lustres. £250–£350

One of a pair of gilded iron wall lights. £125–£195

praying mantis, stag beetle, butterfly and moth.

However, it was the flower that was the most frequently used motif for light fittings. It was interpreted as a stylised design to decorate the lamp. Sometimes the lamp itself became the plant with the glass shades or shade as the petals of the flower. The poppy, blackberry, lily, convolvulus, honesty and all trumpet-shaped flowers were firm favourites with the designers. The other important theme for lamps was ethereal woman with diaphanous dresses or women portrayed as nymphs, naiads or undines. Many designers, not knowing which theme to follow, combined the two, and these became known as *femme-fleur* lamps.

A Parisian, Samuel Bing, opened a new gallery in Paris in 1895 which he called L'Art Nouveau. So successful was this gallery that the name Art Nouveau became the generic term for all the new *fin de siècle* art and the style it generated. He said: 'All works of art shall be admitted which show a personal independence and are in harmony with the spirit of the age.'

Art Nouveau became the most creative period in the history of domestic lighting. Wonderful lamps were created which celebrated the magic and immediacy of electric light. Unfortunately, many of these lamps – although beautiful objets d'art – actually generated more heat than light and were not very functional. However, more and more architects and designers were realising that lighting was the one aspect of interior design that was fundamental and indispensable to every room. A fact we are now beginning to recognise again. Although Art Nouveau reached its peak before World War I, its styles continued to be popular well into

One of a pair of French painted iron wall lights. £185–£265

the 1920s, and are again in great demand today.

· EDWARDIAN ·

The main styles in the Edwardian era were Art Nouveau, Arts and Crafts, and Classical Revival. The enthusiasm for a return to classical styles continued well into the 1920s.

· THE · · CLASSICAL · · REVIVALS ·
c. 1900–28

Between the supremacies of Art Nouveau at the turn of the century and Art Deco in the mid-'20s, was a transitional period of great classical revivals. In England the Georgian styles of Adam, Hepplewhite, Chippendale and Sheraton became very popular, while in France there was a return to the styles of Louis XVI. Great quantities of antique furniture and *objets d'art* were reproduced and forgers had a field day. Georgian styles are so aesthetically pleasing that they have rarely been out of fashion for any great length of time, and these classical revival styles are much sought after today.

Elegant Edwardian brass electrolier.

· PENDANTS · & ·
· CHANDELIERS ·

Small pendant lamps – consisting of a glass shade and decorative brass gallery, suspended on silk-covered flex – were popular as centre lights in many rooms, although the size of the shade was no bigger than would now be used on a wall bracket. The light would have seemed very gloomy by today's standards, although to the Edwardians it would have been an improvement on what they were used to. Often a brass decoration was fixed halfway up the flex; other shades were suspended on a chain with the flex threaded through.

Nowadays these small pendant fittings can look attractive in hallways, landings, cloakrooms, positioned over the dressing table in the bedroom or suspended in a corner of a living room to create a small pool of light. Pendant lamps with silk shades or circular brass rims with fabric skirts similar to those used on gas mantles were also popular at that time. Usually the fabric skirts will need to be replaced, but this is relatively easy and means that the new skirt will match other furnishings. These were often attached to Rise and Fall mechanisms.

Edwardian brass fringed pendant lamp.

Blue peardrop five-tier chandelier. £300–£550

Edwardian centre bowl
painted with convolvulus,
with bronze fittings.
£85–£155

· BOWLS ·

Bowls of cut crystal or alabaster were set
into decorative brass or bronze mounts
and suspended on chains for use as
centre lights in Edwardian times. The
bowl diffused the light and reflected it
on to the ceiling. Often the mounts
were decorated with lions' masks, rams'
heads or rosettes. When buying this
type of fitment, always check that the
glass or alabaster is not cracked.
Sometimes you may see the fitments for
sale without the accompanying bowls –
beware, because they do not come in
standard sizes and it is very difficult to
find replacement bowls. They can be
specially made but this tends to be
prohibitively expensive.

· RISE · & · FALL ·

Rise and Fall pendants were made in up
to three light fittings. Two-light
pendants consisted of a brass crossbar
with a small lamp suspended on each
end and a centre handle underneath.
They were connected to the ceiling by
silk-covered flex and a system of pulleys
and a weight, so that they could be
adjusted up and down. They were
frequently positioned over dressing

Single Rise and Fall
pendant with ceramic
weight and 3 yd flexible
silk cord.

tables in the bedroom or over a table in the living room. They are still very popular today. Single pendant Rise and Fall lights were also available. The most common had a cream-coloured ceramic weight, pulley and ceiling fitment, and usually carried a simple coolie shade in milk glass. Other designs were available in decorated ceramics and in brass. The shades were fairly small, no more than 8–10 inches in diameter.

When buying Rise and Falls, always check the wiring carefully, as frequent use means that the wire tends to get frayed where it rubs on the pulleys. If the fittings need rewiring, it is preferable to use new silk-covered three-core wire which is available from specialist lighting retailers. It is expensive but runs better over the pulleys than the modern pvc-covered wire.

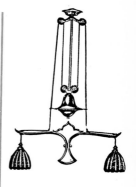

Polished brass two-light Rise and Fall pendant with 6 yd flexible silk cord.

· CHANDELIERS ·

Chandeliers sold for domestic use usually had only three or five arms. The flex was run on or through the arms and allowed to drop down several inches to the suspended inverted light fitting and glass shade. Most chandeliers were designed so that the light was projected downwards.

French chandelier of three flying cherubs, each holding a lampshade of crystal lustres. £350–£550

One of a pair of two-arm ormolu ram's head wall lights in classical revival style, c.1895.

One of a pair of brass wall brackets with large polished back plates and holophane pineapple shades, c.1920.
13 X 7½in.
Pair £295–£395

Edwardian wall lights were mostly designed to direct light downwards, with one or two arms from which the flex was suspended, holding the lamp and small glass shade. These were produced in a wide variety of Art Nouveau designs as well as neo-classical. Designs for gas brackets were also adapted for use with the new electric light. The wall lights that directed the light upwards, using imitation candle lights, were nearly all in Rococo or neo-classical styles.

One of a pair of Edwardian two-arm brass wall lights with bell shade, c.1910. 17 X 14in. Pair £350–£500

Brass picture light made from an old World War I shell case.

floor

· STANDARD ·

These were still produced in much the same styles as they had been at the end of the 19th century. The same designs were used for oil as well as for electricity. Most lamps were telescopic so that the height could be adjusted, and had three light fittings. Sometimes there was a special switch so that one could choose to have one to three lights on at any one time. They were made in brass or bronze or wrought iron with ornaments in copper. As the Edwardian era progressed, designs became simpler and more graceful. Silk lampshades, however, remained very elaborate and decorative.

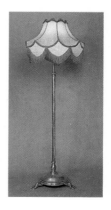

Edwardian telescopic brass floor lamp with round base and claw feet. Period parchment shade.
£185–£295

· LIBRARY ·
· LAMPS ·

These were small standard lamps, consisting of a short upright pole with a side bar (which was often adjustable) to which was fixed a downward-pointing lampholder and small glass or fabric shade. The lamps stood about 4–4½feet high and were ideal for reading. It was made of brass or iron, or a mixture of the two. Library lamps are very popular today as their small size makes them suitable in cottages and small Victorian terrace houses.

Edwardian brass library lamp with hand painted waxed card shade.
£185–£255

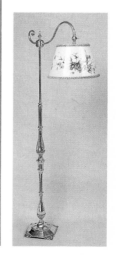

table

Edwardian brass pulman lamp with tripod legs. Note the hole in one foot where the lamp was fixed to the table. This lamp was used extensively in railway carriages and on ships.
£75–£95

· TABLE · LAMPS ·

Brass column table lamps between 8 and 12 inches high were very popular. China vase and figural lamps were also common but they are not as sought after as the brass ones. Silk shades were common in England but glass shades were preferred in France and America.

· DESK · & · READING · LAMPS ·

The desk lamp most collected today is without doubt the Doctor's or Professional's lamp – a brass or bronze lamp with a wide, heavy base and a curved arm which supports a trough-shaped shade in brass or glass. The curved arm was adjustable, as was the shade. Cheaper versions were made in iron or steel and copper plated. Glass shades were usually green, lined white. The second most popular desk lamp has a brass pole and an adjustable side bar to which the lamp and shade are fixed. It is like a small-scale version of a library lamp.

Hand-engraved brass Captain's desk lamp, with relief picture of the Holstentor Gate to the city of Lübeck, Germany, c.1910. £150–£225

Bronzed metal Professor's desk lamp. Expensive versions of this lamp were made in brass with brass or green-glass trough shades. £85–£125

· VICTORIAN ·

Victorian lampshades were usually made of glass or silk. The silk lampshades for table lamps were pleated or gathered and trimmed with frills, lace, ribbons and tassels. Those for ceiling pendants were often a mixture of glass with an extension lampshade of silk gathered and trimmed with swags and tassels. Silk shades for floor-standing lamps were amazingly elaborate, very reminiscent of the ladies' hats of the period. They were extensively decorated with artificial leaves and flowers, layers of gathered lace, ribbons and bows. The profusion of layers of material and the warmth of the electric light bulbs must have made them very attractive to spiders. Spider screens which could be fixed inside the lampshade were sold for the grand sum of one shilling and sixpence (7½p). Small silk shades were used on wall brackets and for chandeliers. Often the edges were scalloped or fluted and trimmed with lace.

Spider screen.

Glass shades were made in cut glass and frosted glass or milk glass and were often decorated with designs and pictures. The most popular types of glass in use for lampshades were: cranberry, opaline, vaseline and milk glass.

Victorian lampshade decorated with artificial flowers, lace and bows.

113

· CRANBERRY ·

Cranberry glass is pale, pinky-red in colour and was very popular in Victorian times. It must not be confused with 'ruby' glass which is a much darker ruby wine colour and was produced primarily in Bohemia. The lovely red lines in both glasses were obtained by adding various metal oxides such as gold, copper, iron or magnesium in varying amounts or combinations to produce pale and dark shades of colour.

Two cranberry lampshades.

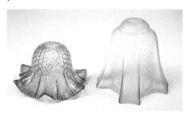

Lampshades were often made of pressed glass with frilled edges; and large quantities were produced in the Midlands – largely for everyday domestic use . However, there are some pieces to be found which are particularly distinctive for their fine quality and intricate design. All cranberry glass is much sought after now and well worth collecting. A small Victorian lampshade would cost £40–£60.

· OPALINE ·

This creamy, semi-opaque translucent glass was produced in France and England from the mid-19th century. One of its characteristics is that, when held to the light, it produces beautiful rose hues. Its opacity was achieved by the addition of tin oxide or bone-ash. It was also made in most pastel colours and special effects were developed by

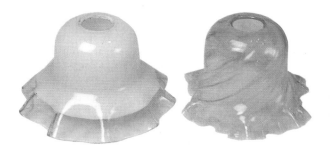

various French factories including: *gorge de pigeon* (pigeon's neck) – a beautiful translucent mauve with grey undertones; and *bulles de savon* (soap bubbles) – a delicate iridescent rainbow effect, similar to that produced by soap bubbles.

LEFT: milk glass shade edged clear.
RIGHT: opaline glass shade.

· VASELINE ·

A yellowish-green glass, similar in colour to the ointment of the same name, but much prettier. The colour was obtained by the use of uranium and varied from acid greens to opalescent yellows with a whole range in between. When lit from within, it produced a warm glow.

Two Vaseline lampshades.

·MILK·OR·
·ENAMEL·
·GLASS·

An opaque glass which resembled translucent white porcelain and when lit produced a warm welcoming glow.

Hand-painted glass lampshades, 1910–20.

·EDWARDIAN·

Edwardian glass shades were very similar to those produced in the Victorian era. Silk lampshades were still very elaborate, although some simpler designs were becoming available. Bead and silk fringing was being used more to replace intricate lace flounces and frills.

Beautiful mosaic glass shades were being manufactured in America, led by Louis Comfort Tiffany, the like of which had never before been seen in Europe. Samuel Bing showed them in his L'Art Nouveau Gallery in Paris and became the European agent for Tiffany, but few were seen in England.

Gallé, Daum, Lalique and others were making wonderful blown and moulded glass shades as well as intricately etched, cased glass and hand-painted shades in France, but nothing very exciting was happening in Britain.

art deco

Art Deco is the blanket term used to describe the many different styles of the decorative arts in the 1920s and '30s. There were two basic schools of thought:

The Sybarites, led by Paul Poiret, who were mainly centred in France and became the heart of the Art Deco movement, expressing their designs of fashion, flowers, fruits and women with a happy exuberance which we still find uplifting today.

The Modernists or Revolutionaries, who wanted purity of line uncluttered by decoration, and were inspired by the aesthetics of machinery. The movement revolved around the avant-garde schools of architecture of the period. In France it was led and inspired by the Swiss-born architect Le Corbusier. In Holland it became known as 'De Stijl' and was led by Van Doesburg, 1917–31. In Germany the 'Bauhaus' movement, 1918–32, was established by Walter Gropius and included famous artists and craftsmen such as Klee, Brewer, Moholy Nagy, Ferninger and Kandinsky. In Italy it was known as the Futurist movement and followed the teaching of Marinetti.

The famous 'Exposition Internationale des Arts Decoratifs et Industriels Modernes', held in Paris in 1925, is the date usually given as the beginning of Art Deco. It was certainly the first time it was accepted and presented to the world as a new art form, but many designs created as early as 1895 had far more in keeping with the Art Deco movement than with Art Nouveau, although they were featured in Samuel Bing's exhibition.

The designs of the Sybarites epitomised the gaiety and frivolity of the Bright Young Things of the 1920s, while the Modernist movement reached

Art Deco carved wood table lamp with lampshade of parachute material, c.1925. £45–£95

Oak and maple Art Deco table lamp with original parchment shade. £45–£65

art deco

French Art Deco table lamp with enamelled glass shade, c.1920. £175–£295

French spelter pierrot lamp with replacement leaded irridescent glass shade, c.1925. £185–£245

its fullest potential in the '30s after the Great Depression of 1929.

Paris led the world of art and fashion in the 1920s and Art Deco was largely initiated and inspired by fashion designers, as is interior decoration today.

In 1909 Diaghilev brought the Russian ballet to Paris and it became a major influence on the new art movement. From then on French Art Nouveau designs began to end and styles became more formalised and geometric.

The discovery of Tutankhamun's tomb in 1922 made Egyptian designs very popular, especially those based on the pyramid.

The geometric and stylised designs of the American Indians, Aztecs and Incas, also greatly influenced Art Deco designers, as is seen in the many zig-zag patterns and stepped designs.

A favourite theme for Art Deco statue table lamps was a fashionable stylised woman in an athletic or dance pose, full of movement, supporting a globe that could be illuminated. Other popular subjects and motifs were: leaping gazelles, borzoi dogs, greyhounds and poirets. Geometric patterns of all sorts were common and all human forms were dramatically stylised. One of the most favourite motifs was the stylised sun-ray. Pure geometry and stark symmetry advocating the aesthetics of the machine became the mania of the '30s. The new materials used by the designers were aluminium, tubular steel, Bakelite and other early plastics, onyx, marble, crystal, pressed glass, plywood and flashy wood veneers.

The machine was admired and respected in this period and artists started to adapt designs to the requirements of mass production, which enabled Art Deco to become such a universal style.

Industrialists began to appreciate the value of good design and big department stores in Paris employed famous designers to open departments for them. Louis Süe and André Mare started the Compagnie des Arts. Paul Follet worked for the Bon Marché, Marcel Dufrène for Galleries Lafayette and at Printemps there was L'Atelier Primavera. Other European capitals copied France's example.

After World War I there were smaller apartments and houses and far fewer servants. There was a big housebuilding programme and new, small semi-detached modern suburban houses sprang up with amazing speed. All space became valuable and to utilise it effectively it needed to be designed. Interior designers came into their own. In the home, kitchens were no longer the domain of cooks and maids. They were part of the modern home, and many people spent time in them, even if they had servants. They had to be practical, well lit and pleasantly designed. Bathrooms took on a completely new look with streamlined chrome fittings, new floor and wall coverings, and particular attention was paid to the new electric lighting.

Designers created an endless variety of chandeliers, wall lights, floor lights and decorative table lamps. Uplighters, downlighters, subdued lighting, architectural and hidden lighting, directional lighting – all showed the many skills of leading designers that by courtesy of mass production were not only for the rich but for the expanding middle classes as well.

Artists used electric light as an applied medium. Art Nouveau designers allowed the light to shine through multi-coloured shades like

Brass barley-twist lamp with hand painted Egyptian scene on the shade, c.1928. £65–£115

French silvered brass chandelier with pâte-de-verre centre bowl and shades. £180–£295

French Art Deco silver
plated brass chandelier
with beaded glass shades,
c.1925. £395–£575

Tiffany's to enhance the colour and
light of the glass itself. Art Deco
designers used glass to direct the light in
a particular way or to contain it in
geometric patterns, playing with the
light itself.

Not all designs and styles
manufactured in the 1920s and '30s can
be called Art Deco, just as not all items
designed at the turn of the century were
Art Nouveau. Classical styles remained
popular right through to the '20s and
into the '30s. Certain designs, in
particular Rise and Fall pendants,
flounced pendants and Professional desk
lamps, brought out before World War I
were so effective in their construction
and design that they continued to be
made for the next two decades. Britain
still had a large Empire and people
living in the dominions were often
several years, even a decade, behind the
fashionable styles paraded in Paris and
London. In antique markets and fairs
and even in shops, items tend to be
dated according to the time their design
was first fashionable, even though they
may have been produced many years
afterwards.

Art Deco was very concerned with a
totally integrated look, therefore a
design that was successful for a pendant
light would be adapted for wall brackets
as well. Chandeliers were produced
with matching wall lights.

Brass three-light pendant
uplighter with marbled
glass shades, c.1930.
£55–£125

· PENDANTS · & · CHANDELIERS ·

Art Deco design was particularly involved with diffused light. Interior decoration had become much lighter and brighter with pale ceilings and walls to help give the illusion of space and light.

· GLASS · BOWLS ·

One of the most enduring memories people have of the '30s is the centre glass bowl, suspended from the ceiling by three chains. Bowls were also used in Edwardian times but then they were a much more elegant style, often shallower or more subtly curved. The glass bowls of the 1930s were very bulky. They came in several sizes, the most popular being about 14 inches in diameter. They were frequently made of flakestone glass and decorated with hand-painted or transfer-printed patterns of flowers, fruit or geometric designs. There were cone-shaped bowls, hexagonal, stepped designs as well as long panel shapes. They were fixed to the ceiling by a metal ceiling plate with three hooks and a centre hole for the flex. These bowls are now becoming very popular again. Vast numbers were manufactured and it is still possible to find examples of the common designs for less than £20 but special shapes and designs can cost £65 or more.

· PANEL · FITTINGS ·

Panel fittings came in pendant fittings with matching wall lights. Both directed the light upwards. The panels were either of thick, frosted, moulded glass

Moulded glass ceiling light, c.1925. £145–£195

Ceiling bowl, hand-painted with swallows, c.1930. £65–£95

often in the design of stylised sea shells, fans or Aztec patterns, or they were simple panels of plate glass cut in different shapes that either slotted together to make a flower shape or fitted into panels in a metal frame. The panels could be had in several colours or tinted at the edges only. Often the colour was applied to the glass as a type of paint. All ceiling panel fittings were suspended by decorative chains. The wall fittings were all uplighters and the panels contained in metal frames.

Panel glass and metal pendant lamp, c.1928.
£65–£125

· CYLINDER ·
· FITTINGS ·

These were pendant and wall fittings in antique brass or chrome with the light bulb contained in a glass cylindrical shade. The pendants usually had three arms and the cylinders faced upwards while the wall lights usually consisted of a single upright cylinder.

· TUBULAR ·
· FITTINGS ·

The forerunners of modern strip lights were long tubular light bulbs about 10–12 inches in length and 1–1½ inches in diameter, with a bayonet fitting at one

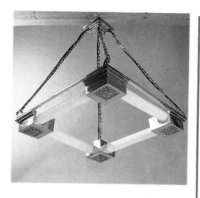

Chrome ceiling pendant, using tubular bayonet fitting bulbs, c.1930. £125–£195

end and a conical tip at the other. They came in 40 and 60 watts and gave a non-glare pleasing glow. They were used with chrome or bronzed fittings without shades. Pendants usually consisted of three vertical bulbs, although square fittings supporting four horizontal bulbs were also made. Vertical wall brackets were placed on either side of a mirror, with horizontal versions placed above the dressing table or over a bathroom mirror. Philips are now producing these bulbs again, but they are only available from specialist lighting retailers.

· LANTERNS ·

Small lanterns of every shape and pattern were produced in great numbers in the 1920s and '30s to fulfil the ever-increasing demand for hall and landing lights. They were often made cheaply in oxidised metal with frosted or tinted glass or 'marbloid' panels. Sometimes the panels were painted with geometric patterns but usually they were plain or shaded. They can still be found quite cheaply, from £8 to £25 in antique fairs and markets and still look attractive in today's hallways.

Leaded glass lantern, c.1930. £35–£65

One of a pair of moulded glass Odeon-style uplighters in chrome casings. Centre pendants were often made to match these wall lights.
Pair £125–£165

· UPLIGHTERS ·

The most popular wall lights in the 1930s were uplighters. They were usually made of concave glass in a semi-circular shape, or of moulded or panelled glass in a metal frame which was frequently chromed or bronzed. Those produced in the 1920s tended to be of a more delicate design, whereas later versions became progressively chunkier and more stylised. The cinemas, especially the Odeon, played an important part in popularising this type of lighting, as they embraced the functional Art Deco styles and installed them in all their local picture-houses.

One of a pair of shaped and transfer-printed glass uplighters with brass mounts, c.1920.
Pair £125–£195

Oxidised-brass adjustable swivel-arm Gentleman's library lamp with original leatherette shade, c.1925.
£395–£550

· FLOOR · LAMPS ·

Floor-standing uplighters were very fashionable and they usually had a glass shade like a bowl or pudding basin which held the lamp and deflected the light upwards. However, many people had conventional floor standards in brass or bronze, turned wood, decorative lacquerware and chromium plate. The designs had become much bolder, with wood and metal being mixed or oak carved in geometric stepped patterns.

Lampshades in huge geometric shapes with hand-painted modernist patterns and long stepped fringing were commonplace on the standard bases. They were made in silk and imitation vellum, using the new translucent plastics such as marbloid, pearlight and Bakelite. The shades were decorated with fringing four inches or more in length and with beads and tassels.

· TABLE · LAMPS ·

Classical styles continued to be
produced in considerable numbers, as
well as the modern geometric archetypal
Art Deco designs. Chromium-plated
lamps continued in popularity, as did
wood and those made in the new early
plastics.

Brass Art Deco table lamp
and original shade, c.1930.
£65–£125

· BAKELITE ·

Bakelite was one of the first synthetic
plastics made from phenolic resin. It is
now a generic term used for all items
made of phenolic resin. It was
discovered in 1907 by a Belgian
chemist, Leo Baekeland.

Initially it was considered an exotic
enough material to be used for
jewellery. Famous jewellers such as
Cartier combined it with precious stones
and metals. At first it was a very hard
and brittle substance but it was
discovered that by adding wood, flour or
other fibres, it became more resilient.
These added fibres gave Bakelite its
characteristic mottled appearance. It was
used extensively in the electrical
industry – for lampholders, fitments,
plugs, and casings for lamps and radios.
Later it was used for all manner of
household goods.

Moulded amber glass-lady
lamp with hand-painted
parchment shade, c.1920.
£85–£135

Tall brass barley-twist lamp
and original shade.
£65–£110

Art Deco painted spelter
lady lamp, c.1920,
probably Canadian.
£145–£175

Bakelite was most commonly made in dark brown for the electrical goods, but it was also produced in black, dark green, blue and red. After 1924 paler colours were introduced and also marbled and striated effects. Complete lamps were made of Bakelite and other plastics and these have become very collectable. They are very light and, unless specifically weighted, are easily knocked over.

·ART·DECO·
·FIGURE·
·LAMPS·

Art Deco figure lamps were produced in vast quantities in the 1920s and '30s, mainly in Paris and Vienna. Many were signed by the artists involved. The bronze was sometimes cold painted and the ivory was nearly always hand carved so that no two figures were absolutely identical. This mixture of bronze and ivory is sometimes called chryselephantine sculpture.

Cheaper models were often mass produced in painted spelter, plaster or a mixture of spelter and ivorine, and these are still worth collecting. A great many artists were employed to produce these statues. Some names to look for include: Bouraine, D. Chiparus, C. Colinet, Ferdinand Preiss, Bruno Zack, Lorenzl, Limousin, Poertzler, A. Boucher, and Le Verrier.

Many modern reproductions now appear on the market and may be passed off as originals. The bronze is often cast in an original mould but the fakers find it hard to join the ivory to the bronze in a smooth, neat way; the ivory faces and hands are crudely carved or not made of ivory at all but moulded out of ivorine.

Many of the desk lamps which first appeared in Edwardian catalogues were still in demand in the '20s and '30s, especially the Professional desk lamps with trough shades and the small multi-positionable 'Adjusto-Lite'.

· THE ·
· ADJUSTO-LITE ·

This neat little adjustable lamp was patented in America *c.* 1911 and remained popular for several decades. Its base consisted of a large felt-lined metal clamp which could be attached to any surface such as a desk or work table. It had a semi-circular reflector metal shade and is now often used as an unusual picture light.

· THE ·
· JUNIORLITE ·

This was another compact, adjustable, metal desk lamp with a spring clamp hidden in its base, with a mushroom-shaped metal shade which appeared around 1930.

· FLEXOLET ·

Flexo and Flexolet were desk lamps with a heavy base in weighted brass or cast iron with a long curving arm made

Brass desk light with moulded glass shade, c.1930. £60–£85

Brass Adjustolite, c.1911. £45–£85

Brass Flexolet lamp with cast-iron base, c.1912. £45–£85

of flexible metal tubing. At the end of the arm they had a metal (usually brass) reflecting shade in a semi-circular shape, or moulded in the shape of a scalloped shell. The most expensive versions were made all in brass. Cheaper versions in chrome or oxidised-copper plated iron were also available.

· ANGLEPOISE ·

The now world-famous Anglepoise desk lamp, used in offices and workshops, was first invented in the 1930s. It is a supreme example of Art Deco at its best. It is a totally integrated and functional lamp whose clean, simple lines look good in any situation. There were many variations on its basic style, and they are amazingly still available at very reasonable prices from £35 to £95.

1930s painted Anglepoise lamp. £35–£65

1930s desk lamp. £30–£55

Desk lamp, c.1930. £30–£55

art deco lampshades

While luxury and designer lamps from France and the United States continued to have wonderful glass shades, a large number of British light fittings had lampshades made of silk, vellum, sheepskin, imitation vellum and the new mottled or marbled translucent plastics. Often, elaborate designs of flowers and birds, particularly parrots, were hand-painted on to them. They were frequently trimmed with long silk fringing in panels, silk tassels, bead fringing or large teardrop beads, in glass, wood or plastic. The shades were often made in simple panelled shapes that people could sew at home. Sometimes old manuscripts were cut up to make authentic parchment lampshades.

· BEDLIGHTS ·

Bedlights first appeared in the '20s and '30s. They were usually made of silk, parchment or plastic, but more expensive designs were made in chromed metal and glass. They were designed to clip or hook over the wooden headboards that were common on beds at that time, and to give a soft directional light to read by. They were often in the shape of a half-cylinder and usually had a pendant light switch.

Brass and adjustable glass bedlight. £35–£75

Bedlight made of early plastic parchment. £15–£35

Jacobean revival

One of a pair of Tudor-style wall lights, c.1920.
£130–£195

While Art Deco designs were in the mainstream of fashion between the wars, there was also a great revival in Britain of Jacobean, Tudor and country styles.

As if to compensate for the Art Deco obsession with the machine, many people wanted to create a cottage or country mansion look in their homes. Hand-worked wrought iron, often decorated with motifs of the Tudor rose, fleur-de-lys, shields and crossed spears, became popular. Carved and turned oak, especially the barley twist and double twist design, were commonplace. Wall fittings imitated early candle sconces in carved oak, mahogany or wrought iron. The light fittings, although made for electricity, had long sleeves of wood or card to imitate candles. Hall lanterns were made in wood with glass or plastic windows, and the favourite flounced centre light was hung from a square or hexagonal frame of fretted wood. Many of these light fittings look good in cottages and barn conversions today. The craftsmanship is often skilled and they give either a warm, homespun ambience or delusions of something grander, both of which are in demand today.

Jacobean revival three-light iron chandelier with Fleur-de-lys and Tudor rose decorations.
£165–£265

using lamps

In the UK a 240-volt system is used, whilst in the USA and some European countries the voltage is 100/110.

· EARTHING ·

To conform with modern safety requirements, all metal lamps must be earthed. As most early electric lamps were not earthed, the electrical fitting will probably have to be replaced with a modern earthed fitting, unless the lamp can be earthed elsewhere, such as at the base. If using the existing fitting, check that the porcelain insulating parts are not chipped, cracked or broken.

· WIRE ·

Old wire can become stiff and the protective covering brittle, so it should be replaced with modern three-core double-insulated wire which can be purchased in a variety of colours. Some specialist lighting shops do sell modern silk-covered double-insulated wire which, although very expensive, will give a lamp an authentic look.

· PLUGS ·

Table and standard lamps should be connected to a three-pin plug fitted with a *3-amp fuse*. Most plugs are already fitted with a 13-amp fuse, so this must be changed to a 3-amp before use, to protect the lamp.

· BULBS ·
WALL LAMPS

Most wall lamps will take a maximum of 60-watt bulbs but for many antique fittings it is preferable to use only 40-watt. For bijoux and very small fittings with tiny glass shades, only 15–25-watt

using lamps

bulbs should be used.

TABLE LAMPS

Small table lamps will generally take no
more than 40-watt bulbs, and many
with small decorative glass shades look
fine with 25-watt bulbs. Larger lamps
with big shades can take 60-watt. All
metal desk and reading lamps usually
take 60-watt bulbs.

FLOOR LAMPS

If they have large shades, they will take
up to 100-watt bulbs; Library lamps and
those with small shades probably only
60-watt.

PENDANTS &
CHANDELIERS

Small pendant lamps will usually take
40- or 60-watt; chandeliers will only
take a maximum of 40 watts per arm
and often look better with only 25 watts
per light. If in doubt about which bulb
to use for antique lamps, always choose
a lower wattage and a smaller bulb so
that the heat can escape and not be
confined, which may crack the shade.

A selection of 1920s
porcelain and pottery
night lights. £65–£195

art nouveau and art deco designers

This is a listing of the most important designers and manufacturers of light fittings who were the trendsetters of the two eras. Several designers first embraced Art Nouveau and then progressed to Art Deco styles. Arts and Crafts was an offshoot of the Art Nouveau movement. (Dates have been included where available.)

a

ADNET, JACQUES
FRANCE (Art Deco)

An Art Deco artist who designed light fittings, mainly chandeliers and desk lamps in the stark functional style advocated by Le Corbusier. His sharp geometric designs made exciting use of nickel.

ALLIOT, LUCIEN CHARLES EDOUARD
b. 1877, FRANCE
(Art Nouveau/Art Deco)

Student of Barrias and Couton, Alliot was a sculptor who favoured the *femme-fleur* theme for his lamps. The light source was concealed in musical instruments, such as cymbals or drums made of frosted glass held in the hands of draped figures. His signature is often misread as 'Allion'. He made Art Deco dancing figures in the '20s and '30s.

ARGY-ROUSSEAU, GABRIEL
1885–1953, FRANCE (Art Deco)

A glass artist who came to prominence in the 1920s and specialised in *pâte-de-verre* and *pâte-de-cristal* glass. He produced small table lamps, often with bases of wrought iron, and shades in muted autumnal colours, with motifs of flowers or fruits in bas-relief against a lighter ground. His *pâte-de-cristal* statuettes sometimes had a light source in the base in a similar style to Lalique or Sabino. In 1934 he introduced

Pâte-de-verre night light
by Gabriel Argy-Rousseau.
Height 6½in.

glassware decorated with gold, silver,
platinum and enamel.

ASHBEE, CHARLES ROBERT

1863–1942, UK (Arts and Crafts)
Ashbee, the founder of the Guild of
Handicrafts in 1888, is primarily known
for his silverware and jewellery. He was
not an Art Nouveau designer as such
but followed the ideals of the Arts and
Crafts movement. His style was
characterised by a linear elegance and
purity of design.

b

BAGUÈS FRÈRES
FRANCE (Art Deco)

The brothers Baguès were based in Paris, although they also had outlets in Brussels, London and New York. They produced reproductions of antique light fittings, particularly Louis XIV and Empire styles as well as modern Art Deco designs. They were particularly fond of using clear or opalescent crystal beads and designed some stunning chandeliers.

BAUHAUS
1919–33, GERMANY (Art Deco)

Bauhaus was an art educational institute and design centre in Weimar, Germany, founded in 1919 by Walter Gropius. Its aim was 'the realisation of a modern architecture which, like human nature, embraces the whole of life'. Its classes, groups and workshops run by famous artists of the time such as Schlemmer,

Bauhaus nickel-plated brass lamp with milk glass shade by Wilhelm Wagenfeld.

Kandinsky, Marcks, Itten and Moholy-Nagy, produced all manner of architectural and decorative items, as well as furniture and lighting fixtures. They were leading exponents of Art Deco styles with clean, functional lines.

László Moholy-Nagy became director of the metal workshop in 1923 and for the next five years, along with his colleagues Max Krajewski and Marianne Brandt, took a particular interest in developing lamps and light fittings in Art Deco styles using the new materials, aluminium and chromium. They were often combined with opaque and matt glass or Bakelite.

The Bauhaus centre was closed on 10 April 1933 by a large contingent of Hitler's police, because, according to Hitler, it was a 'cathedral of socialism'.

BEHRENS, PETER

1868–1940, GERMANY
(Arts and Crafts/Art Deco)

A multi-talented artist, Behrens skilfully applied himself to all types of design. He studied in Germany, Holland and France and became a founder member of the Munich Secession in 1892. He was director of the School of Arts and Crafts in Düsseldorf (1903–7) and became the artistic adviser to AEG in Berlin from 1907.

He was professor and director of architecture at the Vienna Academy (1922–36) and then ran an architectural workshop at the Academy of Arts in Berlin. His avante-garde ideas and thoughts influenced all who worked for him, including the famous Walter Gropius and Le Corbusier.

Behrens was ahead of his time with his emphasis on simplicity and functionalism instead of the flowery

excesses of the Art Nouveau movement.
His designs were more in keeping with
the British Arts and Crafts movement
than mainstream Art Nouveau. Along
with Richard Riemerschmid, he brought
German industrial design to a position
way ahead of the rest of the world.

BENSON, W. A. S.

1854–1924, UK (Arts and Crafts)

William Arthur Smith Benson was the
only contemporary, internationally-
recognised English designer and
manufacturer of light fittings. He was
encouraged by William Morris to set up
a small metal workshop in 1880 in
Hammersmith, London, where he made
a multitude of household objects and
developed techniques for using
machinery to mass-produce good design.

Benson was fascinated by the
potential of the new electric light and he
started to design and manufacture a vast
range of domestic lamps, mainly in brass
and copper, which he sold through his
shop in New Bond Street. He produced
a range of illustrated catalogues and
offered suggestions for specific lighting
effects as well as fittings suitable for
particular areas in the house such as the
hall, stairs, drawing room, kitchen,
library etc. He also sold his lamps
through Samuel Bing's Maison d'Art
Nouveau in Paris.

His designs varied from traditional
Flemish and Georgian-style electroliers
and pendants to modern fittings with
the clean, simple lines so beloved by the
Arts and Crafts movement.

He used silk shades with flounces as
well as shades of various types of glass.
Silk and cloth shades became a very
particularly British addition to light
fittings. He is also credited with

introducing shiny cone-shaped metal shades which reflected light downwards and prevented glare.

Benson is said to be the first to develop his design directly out of the purpose and character of the metal as a material. The form of an article was most important to him and he had no time for ornamentation.

BOURAINE, MARCEL

FRANCE (Art Deco)

Born in Pontoise, Bouraine was a prolific sculptor of sincere realism. He created many Art Deco dancing girls as well as clowns and harlequins, some of which were made into lamps.

BRADLEY & HUBBARD

Manufacturing company, USA (Art Nouveau)

An old-established American manufacturer of light fittings. They are known to have produced oil and petroleum lamps and chandeliers around 1840. After 1900 they began to produce electric lamps, inspired by Tiffany, with beautiful mosaic glass shades on bronze and brass bases. They also made shades of iridescent glass blown into bronze or brass forms.

Gilded iron table lamp with art glass shade in gilt metal foliate framework by Bradley & Hubbard, USA, c.1907–10. 23½ × 21in.

BRANDT, EDGAR

1880–1960, FRANCE (Art Nouveau/Art Deco)

Born and educated in Paris, Edgar Brandt was an artist ironsmith, and at the age of 20 he was already exhibiting his unusual and exciting designs for lamps, chandeliers, mirror frames and fire-grates, through the Societé des Arts Decoratifs, the Salon d'Automne and the Artistes Français. His extraordinary talent with ironwork and the delicacy and technical brilliance of its execution gained him wide acclaim. His iron chandeliers incorporated botanically inspired designs with leaves and buds, berries and tendrils. One of his favourite motifs was eucalyptus leaves and maidenhair fern.

Brandt greatly admired the multicoloured cased glass and *pâte-de-verre* glass which was being manufactured in France at the turn of the century and incorporated shades of this glass in his designs. He made special arrangements with Daum Frères of Nancy and Sabino of Paris, among others, to make glass shades for his light fittings, and vice versa. Although his designs were primarily Art Nouveau, these progressed into Art Deco and his partnership with Daum lasted well into the Art Deco period.

Wrought iron, alabaster and Daum glass chandelier by Edgar Brandt. 32 × 32in.

C

CAUSSÉ, JULIEN
FRANCE (Art Nouveau)

A sculptor working primarily in bronze, he designed many lamps on the *femme-fleur* theme with the light bulbs arranged around the woman's head or body.

CHALON, LOUIS
1866–1916, FRANCE (Art Nouveau)

A highly respected artist in fine and applied arts, Louis Chalon is best known for his bronzes and sculptural lamps. These were often based on reclining ladies, nymphs and naiads, enveloped by flowers whose petals encased the light source. His lamps, like his bronzes, are expensive and fetch high prices at auction.

CHAREAU, PIERRE
1883–1950, FRANCE (Art Deco)

Pierre Chareau was an extremely avant-garde architect, decorator and designer who believed in the sincerity of an object's form. He strove for utility in his work and often managed to create beauty as well. He was one of the first designers in the 1920s to illuminate tracts in the ceiling itself, and to use domed cornices to reflect and diffuse the light. His fixtures rarely come on the market.

CHIPARUS, DEMETRE H.
ROMANIA (Art Deco)

A prolific and talented sculptor born in Romania, Chiparus lived in Paris and

C

studied under A. Mercier and J.
Boucher. His works in the 1920s were
greatly influenced by the excavation of
the pharaohs' tombs in Egypt and also
by the Russian ballet. His Art Deco
figure lamps are now in great demand.
His work was alive with movement.

CLARICE CLIFF WARES

1925–63 (Art Deco)

Clarice Cliff worked as a ceramic
decorator for A. J. Wilkinson Ltd. When
they took over the Newport Pottery,
Clarice designed the warehouse stock
and called the new range 'Bizarre'. It
was first marketed in 1928 and was an
instant success. These early designs
were characterised by simple geometric
patterns and abstract designs in brilliant
– even loud – colours. Although most of
her work was tea and dinner services,
she did design a number of lampbases.
All items produced between 1925 and
1963 are marked in a variety of ways
but usually include 'hand painted by
Clarice Cliff' and 'Newport Pottery' or
'A. J. Wilkinson'.

Clarice Cliff continued to design for
Wilkinson until the early 1950s and

Circus earthenware
lampstand designed by
Laura Knight and
produced in Bizarre by
Clarice Cliff, 1934.
19 × 6in.

remained working for them until 1963, but it is her pre-1935 work which is really collectable and fetches exceptional prices.

CROS, HENRI

1840–1907, FRANCE (Art Nouveau)

Henri Cros was called by his contemporaries the 'man of *pâte-de-verre*' because it was he who in 1884 rediscovered the technique of making *pâte-de-verre* glass, a skill which had been known to the Egyptians and Greeks at the time of Pliny. This beautiful opaque glass is made by mixing powdered glass with a volatile adhesive, and the thick paste is then applied in thin layers in a mould until the required thickness is achieved. The glass is then fired in a kiln. Henri Cros was able to combine the purity of an ancient craft with the symbolism of Art Nouveau.

French Art Nouveau wrought iron lamp with shade of pâte-de-verre glass. The technique for making this beautiful glass was rediscovered by Henri Cros in 1884.
15½ × 16½in.

DAMON
FRANCE (Art Deco)

Damon not only designed and made his
own lamps, but also manufactured
lamps by other leading designers of the
'20s, including Boris Jean Lacroix,
Georges Martin and Daniel Stéphan.
His lamps were designed to be
functional with a sombre elegance. He
manufactured a special glass, enamelled
on the inside and frosted on the outside,
called *verre émaillé diffusant* which was
designed for perfect, even diffusion of
light without glare. He used this glass in
many of his lamps and framed it in
mounts of chrome, silvered bronze or
nickelled copper.

DAMPT, JEAN AUGUSTE
1854–1946, FRANCE (Art Nouveau)

Dampt established himself as a leading
designer of light fittings after he had
designed a beautiful series of orchid
chandeliers and wall brackets for Maison
Beau in 1900. His designs received so
many accolades that Monsieur Beau
promptly had the series mass produced.

DAUM FRÈRES, AUGUSTE & ANTONIN
1853–1909 & 1864–1930, FRANCE (Art Nouveau)

This world-famous glassworks in France
was founded in 1875 as the Verrerie de
Nancy, and still exists today under the
name Cristalleries de Nancy. It was a
family business first headed by Jean
Daum and then followed by his two
sons Auguste in 1879 and Antonin in
1887. They were not artist craftsmen as

One of a pair of wrought
iron wall lights with Daum
glass shades by Edgar
Brandt. The glass was
blown directly into the
iron frame and was known
as reticulated glass.
26½ × 10½in.

d

Daum table lamp with
cameo landscape. Base
and shade illuminate.
Height 14½in.

such themselves, but rather gathered
together skilled designers, artists and
craftsmen to work for them. Their early
work was greatly inspired by Gallé but
gradually they established their own
style, developing their own autumnal
range of colours and special techniques
of *martelage* (a hammered effect), *jaspé*
(mottling) and *pâte-de-verre*.

The firm embraced the Art Nouveau
movement and employed famous artists
such as Jacques Gruber, Henry Bergé
and Amalric Walter and collaborated
closely with Louis Majorelle, Edgar
Brandt and André Groult.

Their *lampes-fleures* were highly
commended at the 1900 International
Exhibition. Although inspired by Gallé,
their electric light fittings showed great
originality with designs on the shades
depicting winged insects, night
creatures, and flights of bats, as if
attracted to the lamp by the light.
Flowers were also used extensively:

d

marguerites, crocuses, columbines, umbels and gentians, all with entwined leaves, stems and tendrils. Table lamps were designed with whole scenes acid-etched in the glass, and frequently the design was carried over to the base which was also made of glass and illuminated.

Daum Frères light fittings are very keenly sought after and fetch extremely high prices at auction.

Daum lamp with conical shade and baluster stem, c.1900.
14 × 6½in.

DESKY, DONALD
USA (Art Deco)

Donald Desky's most famous achievement was directing the interior design of the Radio City Music Hall, Rockefeller Centre, New York. His light fittings in the late 1930s embraced all the modern materials newly available: brushed, satin-polished or polished aluminium, Bakelite and 'vibrolite'. His shades were often of parchment or cloth.

DESNY
FRANCE (Art Deco)

A leading designer of contemporary light fittings for the ultra-modern buildings of the 1920s and '30s, Desny seems to have reached his peak at the turn of the decade. His lamps are essentially architectural in design. His chromed wall brackets, chandeliers and floor-standing lamps were designed to deflect the light upwards and diffuse it, while still concealing the bulbs. His desk lamps incorporated an Anglepoise arm with movable shades and he often made his chandeliers adjustable in height for specific lighting tasks.

D.I.M.
FRANCE (Art Deco)

The firm of D.I.M. (Décoration Intérieure Moderne) was founded by René Joubert in 1914. By 1930 it had become one of the largest studio galleries in Paris. As well as producing their own light fittings, a great number of contemporary artists also designed lamps for D.I.M., including Leroy, Lesage and Le Chevallier. However, by the early 1930s concealed ceiling lights had become so popular that the bulk of their light fittings consisted only of desk and reading lamps.

DOULTON
Founded in 1815, UK

Doulton was founded in Vauxhall, London, by John Doulton. Later he was joined by a partner, John Watts, and the firm became known as Doulton and Watts. After John Watts died, the company, now housed at Lambeth, was renamed Henry Doulton and Company in 1858. A branch was opened at Burslem, near Stoke-on-Trent, in 1882 which still exists today, called Doulton Fine China Limited.

Doulton made oil lamps and pottery gas wall brackets and pendants throughout the Victorian era. Their recuperative gas lights were very elaborate but cumbersome.

After 1900 they manufactured many pottery table lamps, for gas and electricity, incorporating Art Nouveau and Art Deco designs.

Royal Doulton chine ware table lamp with parchment shade, c.1910.

DUFFNER & KIMBERLEY
1906–11, USA (Art Nouveau)

Duffner and Kimberley were primarily

involved in manufacturing leaded glass lamps and light fittings in the style of Tiffany. Kimberley had worked for Tiffany, but nothing is known of Duffner's past. Many of their lamps are not signed but they are of a very high calibre of workmanship and design and would fetch exceptionally high prices at auction. Some Duffner and Kimberley table lamps incorporated a special circular locking mechanism to secure the shade to the base, and this is an aid to identification.

DUFRÈNE, MAURICE

1876–1955, FRANCE (Art Deco)

Dufrène was professor at the Boulle School of Decorative Arts in Paris from 1912 until 1921 when he founded the 'La Maîtrise' art studios at Galeries Lafayette, which designed and produced a whole range of home furnishings and designer items for interiors. Many contemporary designers worked for La Maîtrise, including: Adnet, Chevallier and Bodio. In 1920 Dufrène produced a beautiful range of table lamps with gilded and chased bronze bases and netted silk and taffeta shades with silk tassels.

DUNAIME, GEORGES

FRANCE (Art Deco)

In the 1920s Dunaime produced light fittings for many people including the Paris firm of Edmond Etling and Co. He also won the contract to supply all the light fittings for the ocean liner *Paris*. In 1924 he was awarded first prize for his 'table lamp for an average income home' at the Great Lighting Competition in Paris.

ETLING, EDMOND & CO.
FRANCE (Art Deco)

A Paris firm that marketed a range of small chromed metal and crystal lamps and pretty illuminated trinkets designed by leading artists such as Bonnet, Laplanche, Guillard and Dunaime.

FOLLET, PAUL
1877–1941, FRANCE (Art Nouveau)

In 1901 Follet became a designer for La Maison Moderne in Paris, where he designed light fittings, principally in chased bronze and stained glass, for music rooms, boudoirs, dining rooms etc. In 1923 he was appointed director of Pomone, the art studio of the Bon Marché shop in Paris. Follet also created lamps in partnership with Edgar Brandt and Daum Frères.

FOSTORIA GLASS
Speciality Co.
1899–1917, USA (Art Nouveau)

Fostoria produced fine art glass from the turn of the century and specialised in lustre-decorated coloured glass from 1912 which they marketed under the trademark IRIS. They manufactured table lamps in Ohio, similar to those created in Nancy with illuminated bases of blown glass, as well as beautiful shades for oil and electric lights. The quality was equal to Steuben. Fostoria was taken over by GEC of New York who subsequently closed down the company in 1917.

f

FRANKEL LIGHT CO.
USA (Art Nouveau)

Frankel produced a range of *femme-fleur* lamps and ladies with vines and fruits entwined around them. They also manufactured bronze-based table lamps with bent glass shades set in decorative metal mounts or overlaid with filigree designs in metals, as well as beautiful hand-painted domed glass shades.

FRESHEL, CURTIS
USA (Art Nouveau)

Designed intricate leaded glass shades for L. C. Tiffany, New York, at the turn of the century.

Leaded-glass Tiffany-style lamp by the Scottish company Williams Colquhoun, c.1920, similar to those produced by Freshel.

GALLÉ, EMILE

1846–1904, FRANCE (Art Nouveau)

Emile Gallé was the pre-eminent master craftsman in glass who founded, and provided the inspiration for, the School of Nancy in 1901. He developed and executed with great skill many glassmaking techniques, including: enamelling, often *chamlevé*; cameo glass, also known as *verre doublé*; *pâte-de-verre*; and partly applied, partly inlaid glass, which was called *marqueterie-de-verre* and which now fetches the highest prices.

All forms of decorative lighting fixtures were produced in the Gallé Studios from tiny night lights to table lamps and fine chandeliers. Many of his table lamps had illumined bases as well as shades so that the lamp was not presented as a united entity. Gallé was frequently inspired by poetry and nature and his designs depicted the beauty of flowers, leaves, birds and insects in flowing designs full of movement.

Carved and acid-etched double-overlay table lamp by Gallé. Height 17½ in.

After Gallé's death in 1904, the firm was run by his son-in-law Pédrizet, who concentrated on reproducing Emile's earlier work, commercially and in bulk, and there was little further artistic development. The firm closed down in 1914 at the outbreak of World War I. Gallé lamps continue to fetch consistently high prices of thousands of pounds per item at auction.

One of a pair of cased-glass wall lights in floral bronze mounts by Gallé, under the direction of Pedrizet, c.1910–20. 11 × 9½in.

GENET & MICHON
FRANCE (Art Deco)

During the 1920s and 1930s lighting specialists Genet & Michon produced almost every conceivable form of illumination, not just table lamps, wall brackets, chandeliers and pendants but illuminated ceilings, columns, cornices and friezes as well as tables and vases. Their trademark was a particular type of pressed glass, the ingredients for which were kept highly secret.

GERHARDI & CIE

c. 1800–c. 1914 (Art Nouveau)

This was basically a pewter foundry which embraced the *Jugendstil* movement by employing designers such as Olbrick, Muller and Houistein. In 1870 it started to produce items in Britannia metal, a pewter alloy.

GUIMARD, HECTOR

1867–1942, FRANCE (Art Nouveau)

Guimard called himself an 'architect of art' and designed numerous light fittings in many styles, some of which anticipated Art Deco designs.

GURSCHNER, GUSTAV

b. 1873, AUSTRIA (Art Nouveau)

An Art Nouveau sculptor in Vienna who received commissions from all over the world. He studied in Bozen, Vienna and Paris. His time in Paris greatly influenced his work and he became fascinated by the possibilities of electricity and how this new light form could present a totally new, yet still aesthetically pleasing, illumination. He designed candlesticks as well as lamps which were typified by reclining and curvaceous ladies, leaves and flowers, which held nautilus shell or exquisite lustre glass lampshades. His work was usually signed either Gurschner, Gustav Gurschner or Gurschner Deposé. His charming lamps were mostly worked in bronze with coloured patinas but he also used other metals.

HAGENAUER, KARL

b. 1898, AUSTRIA (Art Deco)

Eldest son of Austrian metal engraver and master caster Carl Hagenauer (1872–1928), who founded the Hagenauer Workshop in 1898, Karl studied under Josef Hoffman in Vienna and after 1919 worked in his father's workshop. His brother Franz (b. 1906) worked with him and after their father's death they were joined in 1930 by the architect Julius Jirasek. Karl was greatly influenced by the Wiener Werkstätte and became a leading designer and manufacturer of Art Deco artifacts, particularly lamps. His figures and animals are full of movement which flows from the simplest of curved lines.

Bronze and leaded glass table lamp by Handel and Co. USA, c.1900. Height 21in.

HANDEL & COMPANY

1893–1936, USA (Art Nouveau)

This company located in Meriden, Connecticut, was owned by Philip Handel of German immigrant descent, and became the Handel Company Inc. in 1903.

After Tiffany, Handel was the most important manufacturer of glass lamps in America and he incorporated almost as diverse a range of glassmaking techniques into his lamps as Gallé.

These included filigreed metal overlays, enamelling, etching, painting and the applying of a 'chipped' frosted finish to the outside of the shade.

Handel produced all types of lamp fixtures large and small, and manufactured his own metal mounts and bases, but it is their glass shades for which they will always be remembered.

HOFFMAN, JOSEF

1870–1956, AUSTRIA (Art Nouveau)

An Austrian architect and fine arts designer in Vienna, Josef Hoffman was a follower of *Jugendstil*, the German/Austrian form of Art Nouveau, which was largely based on the same themes but was a little more austere than the French movement. Although primarily an architect, he did design some interesting lamps, some of which may still be seen *in situ* in the Stoclet Palace in Brussels. He founded the Wiener Werkstätte and directed its operations until 1931. Lamps are signed Josef Hoffman or J.H. Wiener Werkstätte.

HORTA, VICTOR

1861–1947, BELGIUM (Art Nouveau)

A Belgian architect and designer, Victor Horta was a pioneer of Art Nouveau style. His lights were individually designed to be in total harmony with their situation and very few appear on the market as they are still in their original settings. Horta's style was voluptuous and light as air, with twisting and writhing tendrils and bulbs often encased in small glass shades in the form of flowers; thus the lights became bouquets of illuminations when lit.

k

KAYSER SOHN, J. P.

b. 1862, GERMAN (Art Nouveau)

A small German pewter foundry which manufactured domestic wares and a large range of candlesticks and candelabra in Art Nouveau styles, some of which were sold through Liberty in London. They introduced a new pewter alloy called 'Kayserzinn' which had a bright silvery finish.

One of a pair of five-light pewter candelabra by J. P. Kayser Sohn, c.1900–7. 19 × 14½ × 7in.

KNOX, ARCHIBALD

1864–1933, UK (Arts and Crafts)

Archibald Knox's name is inextricably linked with that of the London store Liberty, where he worked from 1899 onwards. He was one of the artists chosen to produce designs for Liberty's 'Cymric' silverware and also for their range of 'Tudric' pewterware, launched in 1903. The theme for the two ranges was Celtic art. He is known to have produced over 400 designs, although they were never signed.

KOHLMANN, ÉTIENNE

FRANCE (Art Deco)

Kohlmann was an accomplished cabinet-maker and interior designer. He produced a wide range of light fittings, including, in 1934, a series of 'Holophane' fixtures. Holophane was a glassmaker who gave his name to a prismatic pressed glass used for lampshades to reflect and maximise the light without producing glare.

LALIQUE, RENÉ

1860–1945, FRANCE
(Art Nouveau/Art Deco)

Lalique was a master glass designer, hailed by his contemporaries as a 'Magician of Light'. He began his career as a talented designer and creator of gold and silver jewellery for which he won world acclaim. Initially, his designs in glass were executed by the Legras & Cie glassworks but between 1908 and 1909 he founded his own glassworks, the Verrerie de Combs-la-Ville. A whole range of vases, lamps, plaques and jewellery was produced. In 1913 Lalique ceased his jewellery activities and established a second larger glassworks, the Verreries d'Alsace René Lalique & Cie, where he designed moulded monochrome glass. It is from this time that each piece was marked 'R. Lalique France', often accompanied by a model number.

Although Lalique designed and created a number of light fittings during his jewellery period, it was only after 1918 that he began to produce a wide range and vast quantity of fixtures.

Moulded glass ceiling light with mermaid design by Lalique.

These included many ceiling bowls, pendants, chandeliers, wall brackets and uplighters, night lights, table lamps and illuminated statues, as well as architectural lighting effects such as illuminated ceilings, friezes, wall panels, and garden lighting. Even the immensely popular radiator mascots for motorcars were designed to be illuminated from below where there was a colour filter so that different effects could be achieved.

Lalique's lighting styles were primarily Art Deco, although he did incorporate Art Nouveau characteristics in his later works. All his lamps continue to fetch very high prices in spite of the fact that more keep being discovered, hidden away in attics all over the country.

One of a pair of wall lamps in bronzed metal mounts by Lalique. Yellow moulded glass with clear cabochons and frosted radiating rays, c.1930–5.

LAPORTE-BLAIRSY, LEO
1865–1923, FRANCE (Art Nouveau)
Laporte-Blairsy was one of the first artists to realise the infinite aesthetic design possibilities of electric lights. His Art Nouveau lamps consisted of amazing illuminated sculptures of luminous fantasies, or *femme-fleur* themes.

LARCHE, FRANÇOIS-RAOUL
1860–1912, FRANCE (Art Nouveau)
An accomplished painter and sculptor, Larche also designed a range of illuminated sculptural light fittings. He is most famous for his illuminated sculptures of the dancer Loïe Fuller who became world famous for her light dances during which she used

158

transparent coloured veils over electric lights to produce extraordinary lighting effects. The whole of Paris flocked to see her and she inspired many famous contemporary artists, including Toulouse-Lautrec.

LE CHEVALLIER, JACQUES
b. 1896, FRANCE (Art Deco)

An extremely versatile and talented artist, Le Chevallier distinguished himself in many areas but especially in the production of a range of very functional lamps and light fittings.

LEGRAIN, PIERRE
1889–1929, FRANCE (Art Deco)

An exceptionally talented artist who entered the field of interior design, as well as designing all manner of small household effects and ephemera.

LEGRAS & CIE
b. 1864, FRANCE
(Art Deco/Art Nouveau)

An important glassworks founded by Auguste J. F. Legras in Saint-Denis, near Paris. The firm produced a wide range of glassware, including a series of table lamps in etched and cased glass with beautiful pastoral scenes or natural landscapes. They used soft autumnal colours, and cameo and enamel painting and were frequently mistaken for the lamps of Gallé. The firm closed down for the duration of World War I and reopened afterwards as the Verreries et Cristalleries de St Denis et de Pantin Réunis. Up until 1908 they had produced many articles designed by Lalique.

Lalique vase lamp, called Ceylan, with four pairs of lovebirds on a branch in opalescent glass, c.1925–32.

LE VERRIER, MAX
FRANCE (Art Deco)

An Art Deco sculptor popular in the '20s who depicted young healthy women in the spirit of the age. He also made a whole range of 'pierrot' lamps, fine ceiling fitments and chandeliers.

Table lamp in cast bronze on black marble base by Max Le Verrier, c.1925. 33 × 18½ × 12in.

LIMOUSIN
FRANCE (Art Deco)

Art Deco sculptor of bronze figures of graceful stylised dancing girls, sometimes made into lamps. His figures were also made in spelter, with the name impressed on the base.

LOETZ-WITWE, JOHANN
b. 1836, AUSTRIA (Art Nouveau)

These famous Austrian glassworks, founded in 1836 in West Bohemia, were bought by Johann Loetz in 1840. Johann's grandson, Max Ritter, took over and modernised the company in 1879, building it into one of the most important and influential glassworks in Europe. With their blown-glass furnaces and refineries they specialised in producing glass with beautiful lustres and multicoloured glass. By the 1880s Johann Loetz-Witwe were making wonderful glass with multicoloured inlays and shimmering iridescent glass. They even supplied crude glass to L. C. Tiffany in America.

In 1899 they showed the world their beautiful glass inlaid and overlaid with combed metallic-coloured glass threads which they called *Phänomengläser* and *Papillongläser*, a glass with shiny, iridescent spots. They were awarded the Grand Prix at the World Exhibition in Paris in 1900. Much of their glass was unmarked, making identification very difficult. If a mark was used, it was a pair of crossed arrows in a circle and Austria engraved on them.

Lampshade and vases by the famous Austrian glassworks Johann Loetz-Witwe.

LORENZL
AUSTRIA? (Art Deco)

A talented sculptor who produced many Art Deco figures in bronze and chryselephantine. It is believed that he worked in Vienna and it is known that he designed ceramics for the Austrian firm, Goldschneider. He produced many sculptures in the 1920s and '30s, mostly of lithe girls dancing or full of movement, some of which were made into lamps. He signed his work LORENZL, LOR or RENZL.

MACDONALD, MARGARET & FRANCES
*1865–1933 & 1874–1921,
UK (Arts and Crafts)*

Margaret married Charles R. Mackintosh and her sister Frances married Herbert McNair. The four became known as the 'Glasgow Four', although they all worked independently and also together. Their Arts and Crafts style with its simplicity of line was greatly appreciated in Germany and Austria, but did not win the same acclaim at home. The sisters produced some fine light fittings, including some particularly attractive 'repoussé-backed' candle sconces.

MACKINTOSH, CHARLES RENNIE
1868–1928, UK (Arts and Crafts)

Mackintosh believed in a totally integrated environment for his architecture and interior design, so his light fittings were always designed to suit a particular room or position. Their stunning simplicity is a joy to behold and it is a great shame that their manufacture did not match the skill of their design.

MAJORELLE, LOUIS
1859–1929, FRANCE (Art Nouveau)

Known primarily for his furniture, Majorelle also designed light fixtures. The metal bases, mostly ormolu, bronze or wrought iron, were made in his own metal workshop in Nancy. He worked in close association with Daum, manufacturing all of Daum's metal light fixtures and lamp bases, and Daum supplied all the glassware for Majorelle's fittings. He also produced a range of table lamps with cloth shades.

MALLET-STEVENS, ROBERT

1886–1945, FRANCE (Art Deco)

A talented architect, interior decorator and furniture designer, Mallet-Stevens was fascinated by lighting and designed integrated lighting systems for his buildings, many of which are still *in situ*. He liked to use the 'modern' materials of chrome, aluminium and steel.

MARQUET, RENÉ PAUL

b. 1875, FRANCE (Art Deco)

Sculptor of Art Deco figures and figure lamps, who studied under Fontaine and Falguiere.

MILLER, EDWARD & COMPANY

USA (Art Nouveau)

Located in Meriden, Connecticut, Edward Miller and Co. manufactured many decorative metal objects for the home, including oil lamp bases, in the late 19th century. As electricity became more popular, they started producing a range of metal table lamps and ceiling fittings with ornate mosaic opaline glass shades in the Tiffany style.

MOHOLY-NAGY, LÁSZLÓ

1895–1946, GERMANY (Art Deco)

Director of the metal workshop at the Bauhaus from 1923–8, Moholy-Nagy was especially interested in developing lamps in simple Art Deco shapes, using the 'modern' materials of chrome and aluminium with matt and opaque glass shades or panels.

MORAN & HASTINGS

Manufacturing Company
USA (Art Nouveau)

Another American company making electric lamps and light fittings at the beginning of this century, with superb mosaic glass shades in a wide variety of designs, all in the Tiffany style. They also produced blown opaline shades and lamps made of cut glass.

MULLER FRÈRES

1910–36, FRANCE (Art Nouveau)

Muller Frères was a family firm of nine brothers and one sister working at various times. Five of the brothers were trained by Gallé, who was the inspiration of the company. As well as producing a wide range of domestic glassware, they also made innumerable lighting fixtures, chandeliers, night lights and table lamps. The glassworks was situated at Luneville and began around 1910. After the disruption of World War I the firm reopened but was forced to close in 1936. The Muller Frères lamps were extraordinarily beautiful with cameo glass designs of flowers, birds and insects, in wonderful colours. Today they fetch very high prices at auction.

NICS FRÈRES (MICHEL & JULES)

FRANCE (Art Nouveau/Art Deco)

The brothers Nics were talented artist ironsmiths who produced a wide selection of ironwork, in particular all types of light fittings, in the 1920s. They used an attractive *martelé* finish on many of their fittings. They were acclaimed by the press as well as interior decorators. They made many of the wrought iron fittings for Daum's glass lamps and chandeliers.

ORIVIT

GERMANY (Art Nouveau)

Orivit was an art metalware company which produced at the turn of the century some extremely fine table lamps in silvered bronze as well as candlesticks and candelabra in bronze and pewter. Their trademark was 'Orivit' or 'Schmitz Edelzinn'. The designer Ferdinand Hubert Schmitz was associated with them.

OSIRIS

GERMANY (Art Nouveau)

A pewter foundry founded in 1900, as Walter Scherf & Co., it merged with ISIS-Werke of Nuremberg in 1906 and produced fine art metalware including candlesticks, lamps and other small decorative items. Sometime their wares carried the mark 'Orion'.

p

PAIRPOINT
Manufacturing Company
c. 1880, USA (Art Nouveau)

In the beginning Pairpoint only
manufactured metal lamp bases and
fittings, but in 1900 they bought out the
Mount Washington Glass Company and
began to manufacture intricate mosaic
glass shades in enormous quantities.
Their fine quality lamps and shades
were in the same Tiffany style as those
produced by many other glassworks at
that time. However, they did develop a
new type of art glass called 'Tulip glass'
which was designed by Albert Steffin
and patented for Pairpoint in 1908.

PARIS, ROLAND
b. 1894, AUSTRIA (Art Deco)

Born in Vienna, Roland Paris studied
under Henry van der Velde and became
a talented sculptor of Art Deco figures
and lamps.

Art Deco bronze and
ivory 'Batwoman' table
lamp by Roland Paris.
Height 37 in.

PERZEL, JEAN
b. 1892, BOHEMIA,
(Art Deco)

Born in Bruck, Bohemia, Jean Perzel
moved with his family to Paris in 1902
where they later set up a glassmaking
business which still exists today.

Although originally trained to paint
stained glass, Perzel became world
famous, designing and manufacturing
exclusive light fittings. His lamps were
extremely modern, highly functional
and designed to maximise the light
whilst still diffusing its rays. He
developed special glass to transmit the
light uniformly which tinted pink or
beige to give atmosphere to a room and
create a flattering glow.

He achieved international esteem and
won prestigious commissions to design
and provide the light fittings for the
United Nations building, Geneva;
Luxembourg Cathedral; the Henry
Ford building, Detroit, USA; the Savoy
Hotel, London; the Palace of the King
of Siam; the Maharajah's residence in
Indor; and the luxury ocean liner
Normandie.

PETERS, H. J.
USA (Art Nouveau)

Manufacturers of leaded glass and bent
panelled lampshades in the style of
Tiffany in the early 20th century. H. J.
Peters of Chicago also produced blown
glass shades with iridescent lustres.

POERTZEL, OTTO
b. 1876, GERMANY (Art Deco)

Professor Otto Poertzel became one of
the most influential sculptors in
Germany at the turn of the century. For

P

many years he was under the protection of the Duke of Saxe-Coburg-Gotha. He shared a studio in Berlin with Johann P. F. Preiss, and there is often some confusion between the two sculptors' work. He produced many Art Deco figural lamps.

PREISS, JOHANN PHILLIPP FERDINAND

1882–1943, GERMANY (Art Deco)

Preiss studied in Paris and worked with Professor Poertzel in Berlin where he founded, with Walter Kassler, the firm of Preiss and Kassler. He was an extremely accomplished and skilful sculptor in bronze and ivory, particularly of Art Deco ladies and of children. They are now very collectable and fetch high prices at auctions.

A painted bronze and ivory figure, 'Flame Leaper' by Ferdinand Preiss.

p-q

PRINTZ, EUGÈNE
FRANCE (Art Deco)

Printz designed and displayed a wide range of concealed and visible lighting fixtures in Paris, during the 1920s and '30s. He was particularly involved with modern architectural lighting and produced some exciting lighting effects that inspired other artists.

QUEZAL ART GLASS & DECORATING CO.
1901–25, USA (Art Nouveau)

Founded in Brooklyn in 1901 by Martin Bach and Thomas Johnson who were both previously employed at the Tiffany Studios in Corona, the Quezal company produced a wide range of glassware but concentrated primarily on their lampshades which were not leaded but made of glass blown into a variety of beautiful flower shapes.

RATEAU, ARMAND-ALBERT

1882–1938, FRANCE
(Art Nouveau/Art Deco)

Rateau was a great individualist and all of his creations were unique, exceptionally elegant, and of a luxurious quality. He was a skilled sculptor in wood and worked for a number of leading interior designers, but his great love was for lighting where his designs often had a distinctly eastern and ancient art influence.

RIEMERSCHMID, RICHARD

1868–1957, GERMANY
(Art Nouveau)

An architect, painter and versatile designer, Riemerschmid was one of the founder members of the *Vereinigte Werkstätten* in Munich in 1898 which co-ordinated and promoted the work of artists and craftsmen in the *Jugendstil* movement. Fascinated by the new electric light, he created numerous table and ceiling fittings. He never quite resolved the design problem of the position of the flex on chandeliers, which frequently added confusion to the overall style.

ROBERT, ÉMILE

1860–1924, FRANCE (Art Nouveau)

Robert was an extremely skilled artist ironsmith, who succeeded in combining 'the functional with the ingenious and imaginative'. He created all kinds of light fittings and chandeliers, the bulk of which were designed for gas or oil lamps. He always used forged or beaten iron in delicate motifs of poppies and

thistles or clusters of flowers with
tendrils for his light fittings.

Émile Robert's intricate and delicate
work was so inspiring that, it is said, he
initiated the renaissance of wrought iron
art that took place at the end of the 19th
century.

ROBJ
FRANCE (Art Deco)

Robj was a Parisian art dealer who
specialised in commissioning many of
the artists and craftsmen of the 1920s
and '30s to make small *objets d'art*,
including lamps for his shop in rue du
Paradis. He favoured the exotic, unusual
and kitsch items. Some of his glass
objects were made for him by Lalique.
He signed his work Robj PARIS.

RUHLMAN, ÉMILE-JOSEPH
1879–1933, FRANCE (Art Deco)

Ruhlman is primarily known as a creator
of luxury Art Deco furniture, but he
also became involved in designing all
kinds of light fixtures, as well as
architectural lighting. His wall brackets
in bronze and alabaster were of simple
luxury designs.

SABINO, MAURIUS-ERNEST

b. 1878, FRANCE (Art Deco)

Sabino designed a large variety of Art Deco light fittings in the period between the two world wars. He used pressed and moulded glass, extensively decorating it with motifs of flowers and fruits as well as more abstract designs of waves, rain and cascades. Sabino designed anything and everything that could be illuminated indoors or out and became particularly famous for his larger creations. He designed lamps for the ocean liner *Normandie* and for many hotels and restaurants.

One of a pair of etched and moulded glass hanging lamps by Sabino, c.1930.

SCHENCK, EDOUARD & MARCEL

FRANCE (Art Nouveau)

Edouard and his son Marcel were art ironsmiths and they took part in the renaissance of ironwork, designing and producing a wide range of items from the turn of the century and between the

Wars. Their skill was extraordinary; they fashioned iron into tendrils, leaves and gentle volutes or roses which held beautiful tulip-shaped glass shades with a lightness that *Art et Décoration* described as like electricity itself.

SCHNEIDER, CHARLES

1881–1962, FRANCE (Art Nouveau/ Art Deco)

Charles and his brother Ernest founded the Cristallerie Schneider in Epinay-sur-Seine, just outside Paris, in 1913. Ernest ran the business and Charles became the artistic director. Together they produced quality glassware and all manner of lamp fittings. Most of the lamp styles were inspired by Gallé and Daum, for both of whom Charles had designed as a young man. The lamps had bronze or wrought iron mounts and were signed 'Schneider', 'Charder' or '*Le verre français*'. Some were only marked with a small piece of red, white and blue striped glass embedded into the cameo piece.

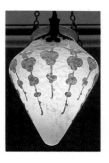

Hanging lamp by Charles Schneider, c.1930. 43½ × 21in.

SECHRIST, ALBERT

Manufacturing Co.
USA (Art Nouveau)

A commercial company located in Denver, Colorado, who were manufacturing fine quality Tiffany-style leaded glass and bent glass table lamps as well as ceiling fittings and chandeliers at the beginning of the 20th century.

SELMERSHEIM, TONY & PIERRE

FRANCE (Art Nouveau)

Interior designers, Tony and his younger brother Pierre won much acclaim at the turn of the century for their beautiful lamps, wall brackets, candlesticks and chandeliers. By 1910 their designs were being produced by Socard and Gallé.

SIMONET, ALBERT
FRANCE (Art Deco)

The firm of Simonet Frères became one of the most successful manufacturers of light fittings in France between the wars, and in the Great Lighting Competition, organised by the Syndicated Electricity Union in 1924, they carried off five of the ten prizes. This success was made possible by Albert's partnership with the talented sculptor and glassmaker Henri Dieupart.

SUBES, RAYMOND
1893–1970, FRANCE (Art Deco)

An artist ironsmith, Raymond Subes had been a student of and was inspired by Émile Robert and by 1927 was considered the best ironworker of the time. He manufactured a vast array of light fittings mainly in wrought iron but sometimes gilded, chromed or decorated with bronze, copper or steel. He used alabaster, marble and frosted glass for his shades and in the early 1920s had a Madame Lehuché-Méry make him a range in embroidered silk.

SÜE, LOUIS, & MARE, ANDRÉ
FRANCE (Art Deco)

Süe and Mare formed an interior design partnership in 1912. Their light fittings tended towards traditional design rather than the modernist themes, and they produced pretty table lamps with alabaster flowers, and exceptional bronze and glass bead wall brackets.

STEUBEN GLASSWORKS

1903–, USA (Art Nouveau)

The Steuben Glassworks founded in 1903 still exists today. They produced every type of art glass, and manufactured exquisite lampshades. The artistic inspiration of the company was an Englishman, Frederick Carder, who as Art Director lent his creative genius to Steuben for 60 years and became, after Tiffany, the most important designer and creator of American art glass.

STICKLEY, GUSTAV

USA (Arts and Crafts)

Stickley, primarily a furniture designer, set up the United Crafts Workshop in Syracuse, New York, to bring together artists and craftsmen working within the American Arts and Crafts movement.

SZABO, ADALBERT GEORGES

FRANCE (Art Nouveau/Art Deco)

Although born in Hungary, Szabo became a naturalised French citizen. He was an artist metalworker whose creations were in the forefront of the design scene for some 30 years from the turn of the century. He worked primarily in wrought iron but also in copper and bronze.

t

TIFFANY, LOUIS COMFORT

1848–1933, USA (Art Nouveau)

No one else has had the same impact on lighting designs as Louis Comfort Tiffany. His splendid mosaic glass shades are known, admired and imitated the world over. He was the son of the prosperous New York jeweller and silversmith, Charles L. Tiffany, whose famous shop in New York sold many beautiful *objets d'art*, created in their own workshops, alongside their exquisite jewellery.

Louis started experimenting with glass in 1883 and in 1885 founded the Tiffany Glass Company. He began to create special effects of iridescence, incandescence, mottling and marbling in the glass. The culmination of this was the creation of his famous 'Favrile' glass in 1894.

When his lamps were shown in Europe, they were an immediate success. Samuel Bing of Maison de l'Art Nouveau in Paris became his European agent.

Tiffany designed his lamps on integrated themes, often plants or trees with the base as the stem or trunk and the shade as the flowers. By 1905 he had over 200 craftsmen working for him in his studios, where he conspired to achieve complete harmony between the various working methods in the arts and crafts.

As his success grew, many people tried to imitate his designs, but no one could quite match the translucent and opalescent beauty of the original creations. It is very sad to find that by the mid-1930s, at the height of the American Depression, Tiffany Studios

Three-light leaded glass table lamp with bronze base by Tiffany Studios. Height 21½in.

was declared bankrupt.

Now there is an enormous revival and interest in Tiffany and his style, in consequence of the value of his lamps has continued to rise since the end of World War II, so that it is not unusual for a quality Tiffany lamp to fetch a quarter of a million pounds at auction.

THE US ART BENT GLASS CO.
USA (Art Nouveau)

This company located in Hartford, Connecticut, was manufacturing an extensive range of bent art glass and intricate mosaic glass lampshades, often with long fancy glass bead fringing, just before World War I.

VAN DE VELDE, HENRY CLEMENS

1863–1957, BELGIUM (Art Nouveau)

Van De Velde was a painter, architect and interior designer, influenced by William Morris and the Arts and Crafts movement. He directed the Arts and Crafts School in Weimar from 1906–14, and became a founder member of the *Deutscher Werkbund*. He designed a wide range of light fittings in the Art Nouveau style, for oil, gas, electric and candles.

VEREINIGTE WERKSTÄTTE

GERMANY (Art Nouveau)

The Vereinigte Werkstätten was founded by F. A. O. Kruger in 1898 as a workshop for leading artists and craftsmen in the applied arts. Its aim was to produce and promote high quality work. It mainly manufactured small *objets d'art*, furniture, lamps and other domestic items.

VOGELER, HEINRICH

1872–1942, GERMANY (Art Nouveau)

Apart from painting and graphics, Vogeler also designed furniture and many *objets d'art* including light fittings, candlesticks, candelabra and sconces.

VOYSEY, C. F. A.

UK (Arts and Crafts)

A prominent British architect and advocate of the Arts and Crafts style, he was a founder member of the Art Workers Guild. He also designed all manner of items for domestic interiors, including lamps.

WEISS, EMIL RUDOLF
1875–1942, GERMANY
(Art Nouveau)

An extraordinarily fine designer of the applied arts including lamps and light fittings. He worked at the Museum of Applied Arts and the Combined State Schools for Fine and Applied Arts in Berlin from 1907 to 1933.

W.M.F.
(WÜRTTEMBERGISCHE METALLWARENFABRIK)
GERMANY (Art Nouveau)

Founded in 1853 by Daniel Straub, this company was originally called Straub & Schweitzer, then Straub & Son, but after 1888, when it had amalgamated with Ritter, it became W.M.F. It manufactured a vast range of small domestic items and *objets d'art* in silver, nickel, pewter and brass. Before 1900, the designs were conservative, featuring Rococo and neo-renaissance styles, but after the turn of the century they concentrated almost exclusively on Art Nouveau designs. They produced a large number of candlesticks and candelabra, as well as some silvered metal table lamps.

WIENER WERKSTÄTTE
1903–, AUSTRIA (Art Nouveau)

It was set up to provide workshops for the manufacture and promotion of quality *objets d'art*, as well as creating complete domestic interiors. Founded by Josef Hoffman and Koloman Moser in 1903, it included leading artists such as Michael Powolny, Gustav Klimt and Dagobert Peche.

Wiener Werkstätte brass chandelier designed by Otto Prutscher, c.1920. Height 45in.

glossary

ACID ENGRAVING/ETCHING: Acid is used on glass or silver to give the effect of true engraving but with shallower lines.

ALLOY: A combination of two or more metals.

ALTERNATING CURRENT (AC): Electrical current which changes its polarity from positive to negative at a frequency (in the British system) of 50 cycles a second.

AMP – AMPERE (A): A measurement of the flow of electricity through a circuit or appliance.

ANODISE: To coat a metal (usually copper or brass) with a protective oxide film by electro deposition, to protect the underlying metal from tarnishing.

ARCHITECTURAL LIGHTING: Recessed or hidden lighting to illuminate ceilings, walls, niches or architectural features.

BACKPLATE: Metal or wooden plate used to fix lights and sconces to the wall or ceiling. Frequently a round wooden backplate was used to fix gas lights.

BAKELITE: One of the first synthetic plastics made from phenolic resin. It is now a generic term used for all items made of phenolic resin. Very popular in the 1920s and '30s.

BARLEY TWIST: A column with a continuous upward twist like barley twist candy, which became very popular between the wars.

BAYONET FITTING: Light fitting to take a bulb, against spring pressure and turned so that the two small prongs on either side of the bulb engage in slots in the socket. It is the most common light fitting in use today, in two sizes, BC (standard) and SBC (small).

BIJOUX: Tiny wall gas brackets for inverted incandescent mantles.

BLOWN MOULDED: Objects made by blowing molten glass into a metal mould.

BRASS: An alloy predominantly of copper, with the addition of zinc and sometimes lead or tin. Very old brass may have as much as 12 per cent tin but Regency and Victorian brass had only 1 per cent tin. Modern brass is an alloy of copper and zinc containing more than 50 per cent copper. Brass containing less then 35 per cent zinc is used for most engineering materials requiring forging, whereas brass containing 35–45 per cent zinc is used for hot working and extrusion. Brass containing 45–50 per cent zinc is used for castings.

BRONZE: An alloy, predominantly of copper with additions of tin and sometimes lead and zinc, in varying proportions. Over the centuries these proportions have often changed. Bronze always contains tin and some contains as much as 21.5 per cent. The usual proportions are: 1–1.5 per cent lead, 5–11 per cent zinc, up to 21.5 per cent tin and the balance copper.

BRONZED METAL: Any metal, but usually brass or spelter, chemically treated to give a brown finish resembling bronze.

CAMEO GLASS: Coloured glass overlaid with one or more very thin layers of other coloured glass, which is then acid-etched or engraved so that the different colours show through in cameo. Sometimes glassware is painted or stencilled to imitate cameo glass.

CANDELA: Basic SI unit of luminous intensity; the intensity in a perpendicular direction of a surface of 1/600 000 square metres of a black body at the temperature of freezing platinum under the pressure of 101 325 newtons per square metre.

CANDLE EXTINGUISHER: A metal, usually brass, hood with a short or a long handle.

CANDLE SNUFFER: A scissors-like metal implement with a small box on one blade for snuffing out candles and trimming the wick.

CANDLEBEAM: Medieval name for a chandelier of two to six horizontal arms (usually wood but also in brass or latten) criss-crossing each other with metal prickets and cups or candle sockets.

CANDLEPOWER: A basic measure of light, which came into being in the 18th century when spermaceti started to be used for candles, which gave a brighter light than wax or tallow. One candlepower represented the amount of illumination in a given direction obtained from a single spermaceti candle. This basic light measurement is now expressed in candelas.

CANDLEWOOD: The resinous wood of any of several trees used for torches and candle substitutes, e.g. bog, pine.

CASED GLASS: Glass overlaid with one or more colours, the paler colour usually white, cut away to show the colour beneath. Also called 'flashed' glass.

CAST: A solid metal object made in a mould.

CAST IRON: An ancient technique of foundry work, using iron with a high carbon content. Although very heavy, it has much less tensile strength than wrought iron, and is much cheaper.

CHAMPLEVÉ: A decorative design is chased, stamped or cast on to a metal object, and the indentations are then filled with enamel.

CHANDELIER: A light fitting suspended from the ceiling with two or more arms with a light source at the end of each arm. It can be made of any material including metal, crystal, wood or china.

CHANDLER: Candle-maker.

CHARDER: A trademark of Charles Schneider.

CHIMNEY: A cylindrical glass with a bulbous section, open at each end, used inside the globe or silk shade on oil lamps and some gas fittings.

CHINOISERIE: Refers to anything designed in an oriental style and pattern. It frequently describes Chinese or Japanese lacquerwork. Chinoiserie was very popular in the 1920s.

CHRYSELEPHANTINE SCULPTURE: A sculpture in ivory and bronze or ivory and a precious metal. Frequently used to describe Art Deco statues.

glossary

CRANBERRY GLASS: A pretty rosy-pink blown-moulded Victorian glass which now fetches high prices.

CRAQUELÉ GLASS: A thick glass with a crackled outside finish often used to make ball globes for Art Deco figure lamps.

DIRECT CURRENT: An electrical current of constant polarity and magnitude.

DIRECTOIRE: French fashion style that originated 1795–9, favouring severe classical lines, similar to early Regency.

DISTRESSED: A trade term used to describe a damaged piece of furniture. Also used by interior designers to describe a modern object that has been artificially aged to give an antique effect.

DOCTOR'S LAMP: A desk lamp usually in brass, with a horizontal trough-shaped swivel shade in metal or green glass.

EBONISED: Painted or stained to resemble ebony. Real ebony objects are usually impressed 'Real ebony'.

EDISON SCREW: The fitting on a lamp where the bulb is screwed into a socket. It was invented by Thomas Alva Edison, and comes in two sizes – standard and small.

ELECTROLIER: A chandelier specifically made for use with electricity as the power source. A term used when candle, oil or gas were the common illuminants.

EMBOSSING: Sheet metal, hammered and punched on a bed of pitch to produce a raised relief decoration. Also known a repoussé.

EMPIRE STYLE: *c.* 1799–1815 but continued into 1820s, associated with the style of Napoleon, often using military motifs, it was more ornate than Directoire with definite neo-classical features.

ENAMEL: Opaque and coloured glass which is fused to the surface of other glass, ceramics or metals, such as copper or brass, to produce a raised design.

FACET, FACET CUTTING: Shallow hollows ground or cut in glass (usually crystal) to make a diamond pattern.

FAVRILE GLASS: A wide range of brilliantly coloured iridescent glass manufactured by Louis Comfort Tiffany, from 1893.

FEMME-FLEUR: A common theme for Art Nouveau table lamps which incorporated a woman in flowing clothing entwined with leaves and flowers.

FIN DE SIÈCLE: Implies the end of the 19th century.

FINIAL: A terminating screw-on ornament usually made of brass or bronze which often holds the lampshade in position. Finials are also used at the base of chandeliers, beneath candle cups and to hold ornaments in place on standard lamps.

FLAKESTONE GLASS: A marbled-effect opaque glass frequently used in the 1930s, especially for lampshades.

FLAMBEAU: Used to describe a lampshade made of opaque or tinted glass moulded in the shape of a flame.

FLEUR-DE-LYS: A French heraldic stylised lily motif associated with the Bourbons. It became fashionable again from 1900 to 1930.

FLEX: A flexible insulated electric cable used to connect appliances to the mains.

FRET, FRETTED: Openwork pattern, usually geometric, in wood or metal, much favoured in the 1920s.

GALLERY: A circular metal plate or dish with a lip containing three or more screws, which fits above or directly on to the lampholder and holds a glass shade in position with the screws. Galleries with wings at the top were made for gas fittings.

GASOLIER: A chandelier made specifically for gas lighting.

GESSO: A mixture of whiting and parchment size which is applied in ornamental relief on furniture, ornaments and lamps. The decorative gesso is either painted, gilded or bronzed.

GILT-METAL: Any base metal which has been gilded, but not necessarily ormolu, which is gilded bronze.

GIMBAL: A jointed metal lampshade carrier.

GIMP: A tape-like decorative trimming often used to cover seams and edges of fabric lampshades.

GIRANDOLE: An ornamental wall candle sconce, usually incorporating a mirror. Made in Rococo and neo-classical designs.

GLOBE: Refers to the decorative outer glass shades used on oil and gas lamps, even though they were not always globular in shape.

GOTHIC: A style associated with the medieval German design of pointed arches and pinnacles, popular in Victorian times.

GREEK KEY: A rigidly stylised geometric pattern which originated in ancient Greece.

HARLEQUIN: Italian clown-like character in a diamond-patterned costume, often used as a statue on Art Deco lamps.

HARP: A metal pear-shaped carrier for lampshades. It usually fits under the lampholder and the shade is secured by a finial.

HARP LAMPS: Pendant lamps, usually gas or oil, here the lamp is suspended from the ceiling in a pear-shaped metal frame.

HOLOPHANE: A special kind of prismatic pressed glass invented by a glassmaker called Holophane. It was very popular for lampshades from the turn of the century, because its refractive qualities maximised and evenly distributed the light without glare. The name, sometimes accompanied by a registered number, can be found impressed on the neck of the shade.

INCANDESCENT: Emitting light as a result of being heated to a high temperature.

glossary

INCANDESCENT LAMP: A source of light that contains a heated solid, such as the electrically heated filament in a light bulb, or the heated chemical salts of a gas mantle.

INVERTED: To turn upside-down. The inverted gas mantle faced downwards, whereas all previous mantles had been upright.

IRIDESCENT: A glass or jewel which reflects light in inter-changing colours similar to those produced by petrol on water.

IRON: See CAST IRON and WROUGHT IRON.

IVORINE: An early plastic imitation ivory.

IVORY: Elephants tusks often intricately carved.

JACOBEAN-STYLE: Articles made in the style of James I and II *c.* 1603–88. There was a popular revival of this style in the 1930s.

JAPANNING: A finish composed of layers of varnish on coloured grounds decorated with 'chinoiserie', sometimes called lacquer work.

JASPÉ: Mottling, mottled.

JUGENDSTIL: The German/Austrian form of Art Nouveau as was promoted in the pages of the magazine *Jugend*. It tended to be more austere than French Art Nouveau.

KAYSERZINN: A pewter alloy with a bright silvery finish made by the German company J. P. Kayser Sohn.

LACQUER: See JAPANNING.

LAMP: Trade term for a light bulb.

LEVER COCK: Crossbar on a gas lamp which turned the gas on and off.

LION'S MASK: Decorative motif of a lion's face.

LOADED: Sheet metal or cast metal filled with pitch or lead to give extra weight to candlesticks and table lamps.

LUSTRES: Cut crystal or glass pendant drops hung on chandeliers.

MANTLE: (i) The lacy, chemical tube fixed around a gas-jet to give incandescent light. (See *inverted*.) (ii) The fabric or bead skirt attached to a circular or square, metal or wood frame, suspended around a pendant gas or electric lamp to diffuse the light and prevent glare.

MARBLOID: An early plastic material with a marbled finish often used for lampshades in the 1930s.

MARQUETERIE-DE-VERRE: A glass technique whereby lumps of coloured glass were pressed into a newly-made glass object while it was still soft and warm. Often these inserts were decorated with wheel engraving when the glass had cooled.

MARQUETRY: Decorative patterns on a wooden article using different coloured wood veneers inset into it.

MARTELÉ, MARTELAGE: A hammered decorative finish that was applied to metal objects, especially pewter and wrought iron. It was popular from 1900 to 1925.

MICA: A translucent silicate found in granite which has a milky, pearly lustre resembling glass and was used to make unbreakable lampshades for gas lights. See also SILICA and TALC.

MILK GLASS: Sometimes called enamel glass. A white, translucent glass opacified with tin oxide and frequently used for lampshades for oil, gas and electricity from Victorian times.

MOIRÉ: A fabric with a wavy self-pattern almost like a watermark. Usually refers to a watered silk.

MOULDED GLASS: Glass which has been blown into a mould (blown-moulded glass) or pressed into a mould while hot (pressed glass). The latter has a smooth inner surface, while the former retains some of the patterns of the mould on the inside as well as the outside.

NEO-CLASSICAL STYLE: A style led by Robert Adam in the 1800s as a reaction to the excesses of Rococo. It was typified by vase and urn shapes, festoons, swags, classical animalier and patera. There was a revival of this style from 1900–28.

NEWEL: The post at the top or bottom of a flight of stairs. Newel lamps were lamps that were fixed on to newel posts, but the term is also used to describe any fixed table or desk lamp.

NICKEL: Hard greyish-white metal mainly used in alloys.

OPALINE: A semi-opaque translucent glass produced in England and France during the 19th and early 20th centuries. When held to the light, many pieces produce beautiful warm rosy hues. It was made in lovely pastel colours, often with wonderful special effects of iridescent and translucent colours. It is highly collectable today.

ORMOLU: Bronze which has been gilded.

OVERLAY GLASS: Layers of different coloured glass are fused together and then skilfully engraved to show the various colours through patterns or pictures. Also called 'cased glass'.

OXIDISE: A finish made by covering a metal with a coating of oxide or rust by combining it with oxygen and sealing it, so that they would not need cleaning or polishing.

OXIDISED SILVER: Incorrect name for silver which has a dark coating of silver sulphate which has been sealed.

PAPILLONGLÄSER: A glass with shiny iridescent spots, made by Johann Loetz-Witwe.

PÂTE-DE-CRISTAL: A type of French glass very similar to *pâte-de-verre*, but with a higher lead content.

PÂTE-DE-VERRE: A thick French glass made from coloured glass paste moulded to shape, used frequently for lamp shades.

PENDANT: A lamp or light fitting suspended from the ceiling.

glossary

PEWTER: An alloy composed mainly of tin with lead added, up to 40 per cent before 1907 but reduced to a maximum of only 10 per cent after that date.

PHÄNOMENGLÄSER: A beautiful glass inlaid and overlaid with combed metallic-coloured glass threads, created by Johann Loetz-Witwe glassworks.

PIERROT: A type of French pantomime clown.

PINEAPPLE: Glass lampshade in the rough shape of a pineapple, for inverted wall or ceiling lamps.

PLINTH LAMP: A circular illuminated low plinth for displaying sculptures, *objets d'art* or flower arrangements.

POLALITE: A tube which fits into a candlestick and holds the candle at a uniform height by spring pressure.

PONGEE: A thin plain-weave natural-coloured silk from China or India used for lampshades in Victorian times.

PRESSED GLASS: See MOULDED GLASS.

PROFESSIONAL LAMP: See DOCTOR'S LAMP.

PULLMAN: A brass or copper table lamp on a short tripod base with one foot with a hole in it. It was extensively manufactured from 1900 onwards and was used on trains and ships where it was screwed down to the table.

PUTTI: Cherubs or cupids.

REGISTRATION MARKS: From 1842 to 1883 registered designs were marked with 'Rd' in a diamond shape divided into compartments, each containing a letter or number. These letters and numbers indicated the exact date of registration and the class of goods, metal, glass, wood etc. From 1884 to 1915 the mark was the year followed by 'Reg No'. The first design registered in 1884 started with number 1 and by the end of 1899 the numbers had reached 351 201. From 1916 onwards until 1979 it was 'Reg No' or 'Patent No' or 'Serial number' only with no year. The numbers started at 100 000 in 1916 and had reached over 1 600 000 by 1979. In 1979 a new system of numbering was introduced starting at 2 000 001. Lamps marked with registered numbers are almost always worth collecting, but it must be remembered that the date indicated is the date the design was first introduced, and the lamp may be of a later date.

REPOUSSÉ: See EMBOSSING.

RHODIALINE: An early plastic material used in the 1930s for lampshades.

RISE AND FALL: A pendant light fitting counterbalanced with weights and pulleys so that it can be raised or lowered as required.

ROCOCO: A name used to describe the asymmetrical decorative style incorporating scrolls, cartouches, shells etc. invented in Paris in the early 18th century. There was a revival of this style at the end of the 18th century and in the Victorian era.

RUBY GLASS: A clear, deep, ruby red glass obtained with the use of gold chloride. First made in the late 17th century.

RUSHLIGHT HOLDER: A metal grip with a scissor action which held the rushlight. It was counterbalanced near the burning end to ensure a strong hold. It could be suspended from the ceiling or table or floor mounted.

SARSNET or SARCENET: A fine, soft silk fabric originally made in Italy, used for Victorian and Edwardian lampshades.

SATIN GLASS: A fancy glass made in Victorian times using hydrofluoric acid to obtain a smooth satin finish.

SCONCE: A wall-mounted candleholder with one or more arms with a backplate of reflective material such as mirror glass or polished brass, ormolu or gilded gesso. It was in common use from the 17th century.

SECESSIONISTS: A breakaway movement of young Viennese artists and craftworkers from 1897 which led to the founding of the Vienna workshops in 1903 by J. Hoffman and K. Moser, where they developed and manufactured items in a severely angular and geometric style. They were greatly influenced by the British Arts and Crafts movement, C. R. Ashbee, and C. R. Mackintosh.

SILICA SHADES: A translucent material found in granite, far more durable than glass. In fact these shades were labelled unbreakable. See also MICA and TALC, as they were also called.

SILVERIA GLASS: Lightly tinted clear glass was rolled over a layer of silver foil and then sealed with hot glass and blown into the required shape, which shattered the foil into glittering fragments. An ancient technique that was rediscovered in the 1890s by the glassmakers Stevens and Williams.

SLAG GLASS: A pressed glass using blast furnace waste which was a purplish colour, and mixing it with clear glass.

SMOKE BELL: A bell usually made of metal or glass which was suspended above pendant oil and gas lamps to help protect the ceilings and furnishings from the waste products of combustion.

SPATTER GLASS: An opaque glass speckled with brightly coloured enamel glass.

SPELTER: A cheap soft zinc alloy used for casting statues which were often painted or bronzed.

SPERMACETI CANDLES: Made from sperm whale oil.

STAINED GLASS: A mosaic of coloured and painted glass.

SWAG: A festoon or drapery of flowers, greenery or the like, curving between two end supports.

SWAN-NECK: A gas wall bracket curved in the shape of a swan's neck with the lamp facing downwards.

glossary

TABLETS: On/off brass handles on the ends of chains fixed to a lever cock on a gas light.

TALC: Another name for MICA.

TALLOW: A mixture of any fats, but chiefly those from the suet of sheep and cattle, used to make candles and rushlights.

TELESCOPIC LAMP: A floor-standing lamp which can be adjusted in height because there are two centre poles which telescope into each other. The required position is secured with a screw and wood washer.

TIN: A silvery-white metal, which resists corrosion and is used in alloys to make pewter and bronze.

TORCHIER/TORCHIÈRE/TORCHÈRE: A floor-standing lamp, originally with a bowl to carry the lamp or torch. It cast light upwards.

TUDRIC PEWTER: An art pewter made for Liberty and Co. around 1900 and used for small domestic wares including candlesticks and lamps, decorated with Art Nouveau designs.

UPLIGHTERS: Wall- or floor-standing lamps which deflected the light upwards, particularly popular in the period between the Wars.

VASE CAP: Small curved metal plate used to secure the top of a glass lampshade.

VASELINE GLASS: A yellowish-green coloured glass produced throughout Europe in the 19th century and frequently used for lampshades. When held to the light its lovely hues dance before the eyes. The wonderful colour was created by the use of uranium and varied from opalescent cream to a brilliant translucent yellow.

VERDIGRIS: A green deposit found on corroding surfaces of copper, bronze and brass.

VERRE DOUBLÉ: Cameo glass.

VERRE ÉMAILLÉ DIFFUSANT: A glass created by Damon to give even diffusion of light without glare. It was enamelled on the inside and frosted on the outside.

VERRE FRANÇAIS: The words found on some pieces of glass made by Charles Schneider.

VOLTAGE: Electrical pressure.

WATT: Unit of power consumed by an appliance such as a lamp.

WROUGHT IRON: A pure, strong form of iron hammered and worked into shape by a blacksmith.

index

index

index

index

· ACKNOWLEDGEMENTS ·

The lamps featured in this book are mainly from the author's own collection and the stock at her shop, Magic Lanterns Antique Lighting, at By George, 23 George Street, St. Albans, Herts. Tel: 0727 65680/53032. Colour photographs were also supplied by courtesy of Fritz Fryer Antique Lighting, 12 Brookend Street, Ross-on-Wye, Herefordshire Tel: 0989 67416; Kim Marston-Taylor; Brighton Pavilion & Museum; Remember Antiques; Christie's Colour Library and Phillips Fine Art Auctioneers. Black and white pictures were supplied by: The London Gas Museum; Shambles Museum Newent, Gloucestershire; Harrods Archives; *Authentic Mid Victorian Gas Lighting & Fixtures* Dover/Constable.